CORPSE TALK
Ground-Breaking
REBELS

God is Truth
the way to Truth
lies through ahimsa
(non violence)

sabarmati

1.3¾   MKGandhi

For Sophie, Finn, Ezra, Maisie, Teddy and Alice.
May you grow up strong and gentle.

CorpseTalk: Ground-Breaking Rebels
is a
DAVID FICKLING BOOK

First published in Great Britain in 2019 by
David Fickling Books,
31 Beaumont Street,
Oxford, OX1 2NP

Text and Illustrations © Adam & Lisa Murphy, 2019

Design and adaptation by Paul Duffield

With special thanks to
Tom Fickling, Anthony Hinton and Joe Brady.

978-1-78845-092-8
1 3 5 7 9 10 8 6 4 2

Papers used by David Fickling Books
are from well-managed forests and other
responsible sources.

DAVID FICKLING BOOKS Reg. No. 8340307

A CIP catalogue record for this book is available
from the British Library.

Printed and bound in Great Britain
by Sterling.

CORPSE TALK
Ground-Breaking
REBELS

BY ADAM AND LISA MURPHY

CONTENTS

OLIVER CROMWELL
MILITARY DICTATOR 1599 – 1658

62

MAXIMILIEN ROBESPIERRE
REVOLUTIONARY 1758 – 1794

68

GEORGE WASHINGTON
U.S. PRESIDENT 1732 – 1799

76

TOUSSAINT LOUVERTURE
REBEL LEADER 1743 – 1803

82

SITTING BULL
SIOUX LEADER 1831 – 1890

88

EMMELINE PANKHURST
SUFFRAGETTE 1858 – 1928

94

MOHANDAS "MAHATMA" GANDHI
INDIAN ACTIVIST 1869 – 1948

100

FRIDA KAHLO
MEXICAN ARTIST 1907 – 1954

106

DR MARTIN LUTHER KING JR
MINISTER & ACTIVIST 1929 – 1968

112

OK, SO, WHAT BETTER WAY TO KICK OFF A BOOK OF REBELS THAN WITH THE MAN WHO **SURMOUNTED SLAVERY** TO STRIKE **TERROR** INTO THE HEART OF THE ROMAN EMPIRE.

IT'S THE **REBEL** WITHOUT AN ESCAPE CLAUSE, THE **HARD CASE FROM THRACE**...

SPARTACUS!

SPARTACUS
GLADIATOR
111BCE–71BCE

SPARTACUS, YOUR FREEDOM FIGHT AGAINST THE UNDEFEATED MIGHT OF ROME BEGAN IN **GLADIATOR SCHOOL**. WHICH, YOU MUST ADMIT, SOUNDS TOTALLY **AWESOME**...

-SIGH-

OK, LET ME EXPLAIN TO YOU HOW **TOTALLY NOT** AWESOME IT WAS...

GLADIATORS WERE IMPRISONED SLAVES, FORCED TO FIGHT ONE ANOTHER LIKE ANIMALS FOR THE ROMANS' ENTERTAINMENT.

THE "SCHOOL" WAS A PRISON WHERE THEY TRAINED US ANIMALS TO KILL OR BE KILLED.

BUT I WAS **NOT** AN ANIMAL. I WAS A **MAN**. SO WHEN THE CHANCE TO ESCAPE CAME, I TOOK IT.

I STARTED A RIOT THAT KILLED OUR JAILERS, AND WE MADE A RUN FOR IT.

ANYONE WANNA SWAP...?

ONCE OUTSIDE, WE FOUND A CART FULL OF GLADIATOR WEAPONS...

THAT'S MORE LIKE IT!

...AND THEN, WHEN A GROUP OF SOLDIERS TRIED TO RECAPTURE US, WE BEAT THEM AND TOOK THEIR WEAPONS, TOO.

AW YEAH!

WE ESCAPED TO NEARBY **MOUNT VESUVIUS**, AN ACTIVE **VOLCANO**.

THERE WAS ONLY **ONE** PATH UP AMIDST ITS SHEER CLIFFS, SO WHILE WE STAYED THERE, WE WERE SAFE.

BUT THE ROMANS KNEW WE'D HAVE TO COME DOWN FOR FOOD, SO THEY TRIED TO **STARVE** US OUT.

SLAVES' CAMP

FARMS

ROMAN CAMP

BUT I FOUND ANOTHER WAY. WE CUT DOWN VINES AND MADE ROPE LADDERS...

AND THEN SCALED DOWN THE CLIFFS - KILLING THE ROMANS WHILE THEY SLEPT.

LIKE NINJAS!

I HAVE NO IDEA WHAT THAT IS.

YOU RAMPAGED UP AND DOWN ITALY, DEFEATING ROMANS, PLUNDERING FARMS AND FREEING SLAVES, TRAINING THEM TO FIGHT BY YOUR SIDE.

FROM YOUR INITIAL BAND OF JUST **80** GLADIATORS, YOUR ARMY SWELLED TO OVER **100,000**.

AND YOU WON VICTORY AFTER VICTORY AGAINST EVERY ARMY ROME SENT AGAINST YOU.

IT SEEMED THAT YOU WERE **INVINCIBLE!**

YES... BUT THAT WAS THE PROBLEM.

MY GUYS STARTED THINKING WE REALLY **WERE** INVINCIBLE, SO THEY REFUSED TO ESCAPE ACROSS THE ALPS TO SAFETY.

AND THE ROMANS WERE **SO** **TERRIFIED** OF US, THEY SENT IN ONE OF THEIR **BEST GENERALS...**

MARCUS **CRASSUS**, A MAN SO RUTHLESS HIS **OWN** **MEN** WERE AFRAID OF HIM.

IF THEY LOST A BATTLE OR RAN AWAY, HE HAD THEM **DECIMATED**.

RANDOM **1** IN EVERY **10** SOLDIERS EXECUTED.

WITH HIS MEN INSPIRED BY **FEAR**, CRASSUS STARTED WINNING BATTLES, AND WE STARTED LOSING.

I TRIED TO ARRANGE FOR SOME PIRATES TO SHIP US OUT OF ITALY, PAYING THEM WITH TREASURE WE'D PLUNDERED FROM THE ROMANS' FARMS.

BUT THEY BETRAYED US, TOOK THE MONEY, AND JUST SAILED AWAY...

OH, COME ON. HOW DID YOU NOT SEE THAT COMING!?

WITH NO WAY OUT AND MASSIVE ROMAN REINFORCEMENTS EXPECTED ANY DAY, THERE WAS NOTHING FOR IT BUT A FINAL DESPERATE BATTLE.

I TRIED TO FIGHT MY WAY TO CRASSUS.

YOU'RE GOIN' DOWN, SUCKA!

YEAH? TRY IT!

BUT IN THE END, I GOT SURROUNDED, SEPARATED FROM MY MEN, AND SPEARED THROUGH THE LEG.

I FOUGHT ON TO THE LAST, BUT IT WAS HOPELESS...

YOUR REBELLION WAS BRUTALLY SUPRESSED, WITH MOST OF THE SLAVES BEING SLAUGHTERED ON THE BATTLEFIELD.

AND THE **5,000** SURVIVORS ROUNDED UP AND **CRUCIFIED**.

SO DON'T GET ANY IDEAS!

YES, BOSS.

BUT ALTHOUGH THE REBELLION FAILED, IN ANOTHER WAY, YOU SUCCEEDED. YOUR UNBREAKABLE DETERMINATION TO WIN FREEDOM AT ANY COST HAS BEEN AN INSPIRATION THROUGHOUT THE AGES.

SO THAT, WHEREVER PEOPLE SUFFER UNDER THE OPPRESSION OF TYRANNY, THEY CAN DRAW ON YOUR EXAMPLE, TO STAND TALL AND SAY WITH PRIDE...

"I AM SPARTACUS!"

YEAH. I'D STILL RATHER HAVE SURVIVED...

AFTER THE BEAST-FIGHTS, CAME THE MAIN EVENT, **THE GLADIATORS**.

GLADIATORIAL GAMES WERE ORGANISED AND PAID FOR BY THE SUPER-RICH TO CURRY FAVOUR WITH THE PUBLIC, BOTH TO GAIN THEIR SUPPORT IN ELECTIONS AND JUST TO KEEP THEM FROM REVOLTING.

GLADIATORS ENTERED THROUGH THE **DOOR OF LIFE**, WHICH CONNECTED TO THE GLADIATOR SCHOOL NEXT DOOR.

THE UNLUCKY ONES LEFT THROUGH THE **DOOR OF DEATH**.

IF THEY WERE LUCKY THEY **LEFT** THROUGH THAT DOOR TOO.

BEFORE DELIVERING THE FINAL BLOW, THE VICTOR HAD TO CHECK WITH THE **EDITOR** (THE OFFICIAL IN CHARGE: USUALLY THE GUY WHO'D PAID FOR THE WHOLE THING).

GLADIATORS CAME IN DIFFERENT FLAVOURS, WITH DIFFERENT ARMS, ARMOUR AND FIGHTING STYLES.

SPARTACUS FOUGHT AS A **MURMILLO**, A SLOW HEAVILY ARMOURED CLASS, OFTEN PITTED AGAINST THE **RETARIUS**, A FAST, LIGHTLY ARMOURED FIGHTER.

SO NOT QUITE THE MODERN THUMBS UP AND DOWN, BUT CLOSE...

I GIVE THE WHOLE THING A BIG **THUMBS TURNED**.

IF HE HAD FOUGHT HONOURABLY, THE LOSER **MIGHT** BE SPARED.

THIS WAS SIGNALLED BY HIDING THE THUMB INSIDE THE FIST.

BUT IF HE HAD FOUGHT POORLY, RUN AWAY OR EVEN JUST IF THE CROWD WERE IN A BAD MOOD, HE GOT THE "TURNED THUMB" (LIKELY A STABBING MOTION).

NEXT UP IS ONE OF THE MOST LEGENDARY **LEADING LADIES** OF THE ANCIENT WORLD, THE **BATTLE-HARDENED BOSS** OF THE BATTLING BRITONS.

SHE'S THE WARRIOR QUEEN OF THE INDOMITABLE ICENI, IT'S...

BOUDICCA!

BOUDICCA
ICENI QUEEN
C. 30-61

BOUDICCA, YOU HAD SOME **SERIOUS BEEF** WITH THE ANCIENT ROMANS! WHAT WAS ALL **THAT** ABOUT?

WELL, WHEN THEY FIRST ARRIVED HERE IN BRITAIN, WE THOUGHT THEY WERE ALL RIGHT! AND THEY BROUGHT PEACE AND PROSPERITY.

MY HUSBAND, **KING PRASUTAGUS**, MADE A DEAL WHERE WE WOULD REMAIN AN INDEPENDENT KINGDOM.

BUT WHEN HE DIED, THE ROMANS CHANGED THEIR MINDS...

HA HA! DEAL'S OFF!

THEY TOOK **EVERYTHING.**

PLEASE! NOT MY **DAUGHTERS!**

BEAT IT, LADY. **WE'RE IN CHARGE, NOW!**

AND WHEN I TRIED TO PROTEST, THEY HAD ME WHIPPED!

LET THIS BE A LESSON TO YOU!

FILTHY SAVAGES.

OH MY GOSH! THAT'S **TERRIBLE!**

I DIDN'T HAVE TIME FOR **TEARS!** IT WAS TIME FOR **REVENGE!**

I GATHERED THE LOCAL TRIBES AND WHIPPED THEM UP INTO A **RIGHTEOUS FRENZY...**

THEN I LET OUT THE **HARE** I'D BEEN KEEPING IN MY DRESS FOR JUST THIS OCCASION.

THE... WHAT NOW? THE BIG RABBIT THING?

THE HARE WAS THE SACRED ANIMAL OF THE BRITTONIC WAR GODDESS **ANDRASTE,** AND WE BELIEVED THE PATH OF ITS RUN WOULD PREDICT HER FAVOUR IN BATTLE.

DEFEAT

VICTORY

AND I PREDICTED WE WERE GOING TO KICK SOME SERIOUS ROMAN BUTT!

FIRST WE MARCHED ON **CAMULODUNUM** (MODERN COLCHESTER), THE HEAVILY FORTIFIED CAPITAL CITY OF THE ROMANS IN BRITAIN, KILLED EVERYONE INSIDE, AND BURNED THE WHOLE PLACE TO THE GROUND.

WHAT WERE THE, YOU KNOW, **ROMAN ARMY** DOING ABOUT ALL THIS?

OH, A FEW LEGIONS SHOWED UP, BUT THEY WERE NO MATCH FOR MY MASSIVE FORCE!

It also helped that the Roman Governor of Britain, **Seutonius Paulinus**, was away destroying the last of the **Druids** on the mystic island of **Mona** (modern Anglesey in Wales).

WHAT'S THAT? A MASSIVE REBELLION?

UH, I'M JUST IN THE MIDDLE OF SOMETHING RIGHT NOW...

The Romans were generally pretty tolerant of local religions, but the Druids, high priests of the Celtic religion, were constantly inciting rebellions.

Plus they may have done a teensy-weensy bit of **human sacrifice** every now and then, which always freaked the Romans out.

Hypocritical, if you ask me, considering how many millions **they** killed in their wars of conquest.

BUT THEN MAYBE I'M BIASED...

Anyway, he came rushing back to try and defend my next target, the tiny trading settlement of **Londinium** (modern London).

Except when he saw my massive army, he **ran away!**

IT'S CALLED A TACTICAL WITHDRAWL!

Whatever. We pursued, smashing and burning as we went, until we cornered him in what **seemed** like an ideal position.

We had them trapped in a narrow gorge, outnumbered by **twenty** to one.

THICK FOREST

ROMANS

CLIFFS

CLIFFS

EEP!

ICENI

SPECTATORS

UH, SIR, I HAVE TO GO. MY WIFE'S GIVING BIRTH...

MY MUM'S GIVING BIRTH!

I'M GIVING BIRTH!

Destroy this one **tiny** army, and we'd have **ended** the Roman occupation of Britain!

We prepared for battle...

LOOKING GOOD, NIGEL. VERY SCARY.

HAIR SPIKED WITH **LIME.**

WOAD: BLUE WAR PAINT.

AND THEN, WE **CHARGED**. A **TIDAL WAVE** OF SCREAMING WARRIORS, **HURTLING** TOWARDS THE ENEMY.

SOME EVEN WENT INTO BATTLE **NAKED** TO SHOW HOW **BRAVE** THEY WERE!

BUT THEN, JUST AS WE REACHED THEM...

HEY! NO FAIR!

CLANG!

DEFINITELY NO FAIR!

STAB!

WE HADN'T COUNTED ON THE ROMAN **TORTOISE**: AN IMPENETRABLE WALL OF SHIELDS, SWORDS AND SPEARS.

WE'D BEEN **SO SURE** OF VICTORY, WE'D EVEN BROUGHT OUR **FAMILIES** ALONG TO WATCH...

GO DAD!

WE'RE NUMERAL II!

BIG MISTAKE! AS THE TORTOISE ADVANCED, WE TRIED TO BACK AWAY, AND WERE **PINNED** AGAINST OUT OWN CARTS.

ARRGH!

GET OUT OF THE WAY!

IT WAS A **MASSACRE**. **EVERYONE** WAS SLAUGHTERED.

I COULDN'T LIVE WITH DEFEAT, SO I DRANK **POISON**!

NOW **THAT'S** WHAT I CALL A **DRAMA QUEEN**!

17

MY NEXT GUEST WAS A **CONSCIENTIOUS CRITIC** OF THE **CROWN** WHO WENT FROM **BESTIES** TO **WORSTIES** WITH ENGLISH KING **HENRY II**!

PLEASE WELCOME THE MOST POPULAR **MIRACLE-WORKING MARTYR** OF MEDIEVAL ENGLAND...

SAINT THOMAS BECKET!

THOMAS BECKET
SAINT
1118–1170

ST THOMAS, AFTER YOUR DEATH, THOUSANDS MADE THE PILGRIMAGE TO YOUR SHRINE IN CANTERBURY EVERY YEAR. BUT YOU DIDN'T START OUT AS A LIKELY CANDIDATE FOR SAINTLY SUPER-STARDOM...

NO, ALAS, I BEGAN MY LIFE AS A POOR MISERABLE SINNER JUST LIKE THE REST OF YOU...

GEE, THANKS.

NOT POOR IN THE **LITERAL** SENSE, YOU UNDERSTAND. AS **CHANCELLOR**, I WAS THE RICHEST AND MOST POWERFUL MAN IN THE REALM, AFTER THE KING OF COURSE.

HENRY AND I WERE THE **BEST** OF FRIENDS. WE LIVED, WORKED AND WENT EVERYWHERE TOGETHER.

WE WERE BOTH DRIVEN TO BE THE **BEST**.

AS CHANCELLOR THAT MOSTLY MEANT TAKING PEOPLE'S MONEY.

AND, OF COURSE, CRUSHING THE KING'S ENEMIES, BURNING THEIR HOMES AND STRIPPING THEM OF ALL THEIR POSSESSIONS.

SO WHEN THE HEAD OF THE ENGLISH CHURCH, THE ARCHBISHOP OF CANTERBURY, DIED, AND HENRY NOMINATED **YOU** TO TAKE OVER, THERE WAS **UPROAR**.

NOT **THAT** GUY!

HE'S A GREEDY KILLER, NOT A MAN OF GOD!

HA HA! WITH **YOU** IN CHARGE, I CAN **FINALLY** MAKE THE CHURCH DO **WHATEVER I WANT**!

UH, ABOUT THAT...

HENRY, MY FRIEND, RIGHT NOW I WORK FOR YOU...

AND A FINE JOB YOU'RE DOING!

THANKS.

BUT, IF YOU MAKE ME ARCHBISHOP, I'D BE WORKING FOR **GOD**. AND SINCE I ALWAYS HAVE TO **BE THE BEST**, I'LL DO AN EQUALLY GOOD JOB FOR **HIM**.

I'LL **HAVE** TO OPPOSE YOU, AND WE'LL BECOME ENEMIES.

PAH! NONSENSE! GREAT BUDDIES LIKE US!? THAT'LL NEVER HAPPEN.

BUT IT **DID** HAPPEN. YOU BECAME THE ARCHBISHOP AND SUDDENLY YOU WENT FROM CRAZY RICH TO **CRAZY HOLY**.

YOU SWAPPED ALL YOUR RICHES AND FANCY CLOTHES FOR POVERTY, FASTING AND A **HAIR SHIRT**. WHAT EVEN IS THAT?

IT'S A SHIRT MADE OF **GOAT'S HAIR**, WHICH IS BASICALLY THE **ITCHIEST** SUBSTANCE KNOWN TO MAN.

SWARMING WITH **LICE** FOR ADDED BITEYNESS.

21

I WORE IT AS UNDERWEAR, SO IT WOULD **TORMENT** ME CONSTANTLY AS A REMINDER THAT I WAS A **MISERABLE SINNER** WHO DESERVED TO BE PUNISHED.

THAT'S PRETTY FREAKY...

BUT ANYWAYS, BACK TO THE STORY.

YOU STARTED OPPOSING HENRY ALL **OVER** THE PLACE...

HE WANTED TO **TAKE OVER** THE CHURCH! WELL, THE **BEST ARCHBISHOP EVER** WASN'T GONNA LET THAT HAPPEN!

DUDE, WHAT IS **WRONG** WITH YOU!? I'VE GIVEN YOU **EVERYTHING**, AND NOW YOU'RE OPPOSING ME ALL **OVER** THE PLACE? WHERE'S THE **LOVE**!?

MY LOVE IS FOR **GOD**, WHO HUMBLES THE CRUEL TYRANNY OF KINGS...

DON'T **YOU** LECTURE ME, PAL!

I'M YOUR **KING**! YOU HAVE TO DO WHAT I SAY!

GOD IS **YOUR** KING! YOU HAVE TO DO WHAT **HE** SAYS!

YEAH. THAT DIDN'T GO DOWN TOO WELL...

THE TWO OF YOU KEPT AT EACH OTHER'S THROATS FOR YEARS...

AT ONE POINT YOU WERE GOING TO DAMN THE **WHOLE OF ENGLAND** TO HELL BY EXCOMMUNICATING THEM, BUT THE POPE TALKED YOU OUT OF IT.

BUT THE FINAL STRAW CAME WHEN YOU EXCOMMUNICATED SOME BISHOPS WHO HAD TAKEN HENRY'S SIDE...

HENRY WENT **BALLISTIC!**

WILL NO ONE **RID** ME OF THIS TURBULENT PRIEST!?*

* ACTUAL QUOTE

HE LATER CLAIMED HE WAS JUST SPOUTING OFF, BUT FOUR OF HIS KNIGHTS TOOK HIM LITERALLY.

THEY SLAUGHTERED YOU ON THE FLOOR OF YOUR CHURCH AT CANTERBURY CATHEDRAL.

THEY EVEN CUT THE TOP OFF MY HEAD.

BRUTAL.

KILLING A PRIEST IN HIS CHURCH WAS AN **UNPARDONABLE SIN.** SOON THE WHOLE CHRISTIAN WORLD WAS UP IN ARMS.

EVEN THOUGH HE CLAIMED HE DIDN'T MEAN IT AS AN ORDER, HENRY STILL HAD TO DO **PENANCE** FOR CAUSING YOUR DEATH.

HE WALKED TO CANTERBURY BAREFOOT, WEARING A SACK AND ASHES, WHILE BEING WHIPPED BY MONKS.

ARE WE THERE YET?

AND, AS IF GETTING HENRY TO SAY SORRY WASN'T MIRACLE ENOUGH, WITHIN **HOURS** OF YOUR DEATH, PEOPLE WERE CLAIMING TO HAVE BEEN **CURED** BY YOUR EXTRA-POWERFUL HOLINESS.

SOON, YOUR SHRINE WAS CLOCKING UP MIRACLES AT A RATE OF ONE A **WEEK**, MAKING IT THE MOST POPULAR, FREQUENTLY VISITED AND **RICHEST** IN ALL OF ENGLAND.

AW, YEAH! WHO'S NUMBER ONE!?

YOU KNOW **PRIDE'S** A SIN RIGHT?

THO-MAS! THO-MAS!

23

PILLARS of THE EARTH

SHORTLY AFTER THE MURDER OF **ARGY-BARGY ARCHBISHOP ST THOMAS BECKET**, HIS CATHEDRAL AT CANTERBURY CAUGHT FIRE AND HAD TO BE REBUILT.

WHICH WAS A PERFECT OPPORTUNITY FOR THEM TO **REMODEL** IT INTO A SUITABLY SPLENDID SHRINE FOR A SUPERB SAINT LIKE ME!

CANTERBURY FOLLOWED THE STANDARD PATTERN OF THE NEW **GOTHIC-STYLE** CATHEDRALS...

BUT WITH A FEW SPECIAL **ST THOMAS** TOUCHES.

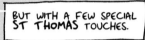

THE **NAVE** IS THE MAIN CENTRAL HALL WHERE THE WORSHIPPERS SIT DURING MASS.

THE **TRANSEPT** CROSSES THE NAVE, TURNING THE WHOLE BUILDING INTO A MASSIVE CHRISTIAN SYMBOL.

UNLIKE TODAY, IN THE MIDDLE AGES IT WOULD HAVE BEEN QUITE NOISY. PEOPLE TALKED, ATE, MET FRIENDS, DID BUSINESS AND EVEN BROUGHT THEIR **DOGS** TO CHURCH.

THE TRANSEPT ON THE FAR SIDE IS KNOWN AS **THE MARTYRDOM** – THAT'S WHERE I GOT THE TOP OF MY HEAD CHOPPED OFF.

THIS IS **EXTREMELY** NOT COOL, GUYS...

EVERYTHING BEYOND THE CENTRAL CROSSING IS THE MUCH QUIETER **CHANCEL** - ONLY PRIESTS AND PILGRIMS WERE ALLOWED IN.

NAVE CHANCEL

SHH!

MASTER MASON **WILLIAM OF SENS** FELL FROM THE ROOF HERE, POOR GUY. INCREDIBLY, HE SURVIVED, BUT HE WAS BADLY WOUNDED AND WAS REPLACED BY HIS APPRENTICE, **WILLIAM THE ENGLISHMAN.**

BE A RIGHT SHAME IF SOMEONE **SLIPPED** UP HERE, EH BOSS?

THE **APSE**, A DOMED CHAPEL, WAS SPECIALLY BUILT TO HOUSE MY AWESOME SHRINE!

PILGRIMS LEFT OFFERINGS OF GOLD, JEWELS AND **WAX MODELS** OF BODY PARTS THEY WANTED HEALED.

AND AT THE VERY FAR END WAS THE **CORONA**, AN EXTRA TINY CHAPEL WHERE THEY KEPT THE **CHOPPED-OFF TOP OF MY HEAD** - YES, REALLY!

CANTERBURY CATHEDRAL IS STILL THE HOME BASE OF THE **CHURCH OF ENGLAND.** BUT YOU CAN'T ACTUALLY VISIT ST THOMAS'S SHRINE, SINCE IT WAS DESTROYED BY **HENRY VIII.**

IT WAS **WHAAT!?**

YEAH, WELL, HENRY WASN'T TOO KEEN ON PEOPLE WHO **DISOBEYED THEIR KINGS.**

HE HAD YOU DE-SAINTED AND CARTED OFF ALL THE GOLD AND JEWELS.

HE DIDN'T TAKE THE BODY PARTS THOUGH...

EW.

REBEL, TRAITOR, VISIONARY, FREEDOM FIGHTER; MY NEXT GUEST IS A **BAD-BOY BARON** WHO **CAPTURED A KING** AND **SHOOK UP THE STATUS QUO.**

GET READY FOR THE **GRANDADDY OF MODERN GOVERNMENT...**

SIMON DE MONTFORT!

SIMON DE MONTFORT
REBELLIOUS EARL
☠ 1208-1265 ☠

SIMON, YOU DIDN'T START OUT AS A **RADICAL REFORMER.** YOU CAME OVER TO ENGLAND FROM YOUR NATIVE FRANCE WITH ONLY TWO THINGS ON YOUR MIND – MONEY AND POWER!

YEAH, MY OLDER BROTHER HAD SNAFFLED ALL THE FAMILY LANDS IN FRANCE, BUT WE HAD SOME LANDS IN ENGLAND TOO, SO I FIGURED WHY NOT TRY MY LUCK THERE?

I SWEET-TALKED THE ENGLISH KING, HENRY III, INTO GIVING ME THE EARL OF LEICESTER JOB.

SO NOW I HAD SOME POWER, BUT I WAS STILL SHORT OF CASH. IT'S EXPENSIVE WORK, BEING AN EARL!

THE MAIN THING WAS, I HAD TO SUPPLY **60 KNIGHTS** ANY TIME THE KING WANTED TO FIGHT A BATTLE.

WHAT'S THAT?

DID SOMEBODY SAY **BATTLE**?

THAT'S **60** GUYS, **AND** THEIR FAMILIES, **AND** THEIR SERVANTS, SQUIRES, PAGES, ETC., **NONE** OF WHOM EVER DID A LICK OF WORK, AND **ALL** OF WHOM NEEDED TO BE FED, CLOTHED, HOUSED, HORSED AND ARMOURED BY **ME!**

OW! WATCH IT!

NO PUSHING!

PLUS IT WOULDN'T DO TO APPEAR OUT AND ABOUT LOOKING SHABBY. IT TAKES **CASH MONEY** TO LOOK THIS GOOD!

YEAH, YEAH, IT'S A HARD-KNOCK LIFE...

SO WHAT DID YOU **DO** ABOUT IT?

I DID WHAT ANY SELF-RESPECTING YOUNG NOBLEMAN WOULD DO...

I FOUND A SUPER-RICH **SUGAR-MUMMY** TO FOOT THE BILL, IN THE FORM OF THE KING'S SISTER!

HER FIRST HUSBAND HAD JUST DIED, AND SHE'D TAKEN A VOW NEVER TO EVEN **LOOK** AT A MAN AGAIN...

I WILL ALWAYS HONOUR HIS MEMORY...

UNTIL SHE MET **ME**, THAT IS.

UH... HAD MY FINGERS CROSSED...

HEY!

BUT MARRYING THE KING'S SISTER IS A BIG DEAL. THE OTHER LORDS WANTED THEIR SAY IN THE MATTER.

WHOA! HOLD ON...

WE'RE SUPPOSED TO BE THE PARLIAMENT!

HOW COME WE WEREN'T CONSULTED?

UM... DON'T SUPPOSE YOU HAVE ANY **OTHER** SISTERS?

BUT ALL THOSE JEALOUS JOHNNIES COULDN'T STAND IN THE WAY OF TRUE LOVE!

TRUE LOVE!? GET REAL!

EARLS CAN'T AFFORD TO MARRY FOR LOVE – IT'S ALL ABOUT POWER, STATUS AND MONEY!

WELL, YOU HAD PLENTY OF MONEY NOW. CONGRATULATIONS.

HEY – MO' MONEY, MO' PROBLEMS... THE KING AND I FELL OUT...

HOW COME?

HOW COME!? BECAUSE HE WAS A BIG DRIP WHO COULDN'T HANDLE HAVING A REAL MAN SHOWING HIM UP ALL THE TIME! THAT'S HOW COME.

HE STARTED GIVING ALL THE LANDS AND TITLES TO A BUNCH OF NEW FAVOURITES...

WHICH IS TOTALLY UNFAIR! THE KING SHOULDN'T HAVE FAVOURITES; HE'S SUPPOSED TO TREAT ALL HIS SUBJECTS EQUALLY!

SO IT WAS OK WHEN YOU WERE THE FAVOURITE?

THAT IS NOT THE POINT.

A BUNCH OF US LORDS TRIED TO MAKE HIM PROMISE TO DO WHAT WE SAID, BUT HE JUST WENT BACK ON HIS WORD...

I'M APPOINTED BY GOD!

ALSO; HAD MY FINGERS CROSSED!

SO THERE WAS REALLY ONLY ONE THING FOR IT: A MASSIVE BATTLE WHERE I CAPTURED THE KING, TOOK HIM PRISONER AND STARTED RUNNING THINGS MYSELF.

UM... NOW I'M NOT AN EXPERT, BUT ISN'T BEATING UP YOUR KING CONSIDERED HIGH TREASON?

NOT IF HE'S A WEAK, CORRUPT DUMMY POO-HEAD LIKE HENRY III!

BUT YEAH, YOU'RE RIGHT, IT DIDN'T LOOK TOO GOOD. I NEEDED SOME **MAJOR GOODWILL** FROM THE COMMON PEOPLE IF I WAS TO KEEP THEIR SUPPORT.

BUT HOW DOES A BUNCH OF BARONS LOOKING OUT FOR THEMSELVES HELP THE COMMON PEOPLE?

RIGHT. EXACTLY WHAT **I** WAS THINKING.

BOOM! **GENIUS MOMENT!** I THOUGHT: LET'S MAKE A PARLIAMENT FULL OF **COMMONERS** TO MAKE SURE **THEIR** INTERESTS GET REPRESENTED TOO!

OOH. HOW'D THE **OTHER** LORDS LIKE THAT IDEA?

YEAH. NOT SO MUCH...

THEY ALL DESERTED ME AND RE-JOINED THE KING'S SIDE.

WHAT!? TAKE ORDERS FROM A BUNCH OF COMMONERS!?

I'D RATHER BE DEAD!

BUT YOU STUCK TO YOUR GUNS...

WHAT'S "GUNS"?

ABANDONED BY YOUR ALLIES, SURROUNDED BY YOUR ENEMIES, WITH ONLY A HANDFUL OF HARDCORE FOLLOWERS, YOU CHOSE TO GO OUT IN A BLAZE OF GLORY.

AT THE FINAL BATTLE, I STILL HAD THE KING PRISONER, SO I DRESSED HIM UP IN FULL ARMOUR SO NO ONE WOULD RECOGNISE HIM.

HE ONLY SAVED HIMSELF BY LYING DOWN ON THE BATTLEFIELD AND CRYING.

DON'T **KILL** ME. I'M YOUR KING!

I'M YOUR **KING**... OO HOO HOO...

TOLD YOU HE WAS A WIMP.

SO I GUESS THE WORLD JUST WASN'T **READY** FOR YOUR RADICAL NEW FORM OF GOVERNMENT.

BUT TODAY EVERY DEMOCRATIC COUNTRY IN THE **WORLD** USES A VERSION OF YOUR SYSTEM, WITH REPRESENTATIVES OF **ALL** THE **PEOPLE** MAKING UP THE PARLIAMENT.

I GUESS YOU WERE JUST TOO **EARLY**.

GEDDIT?

EARL-Y

'COS YOU'RE AN... EARL?

OH LORDY!

29

NOW LET'S MEET THE MAN WHO GAVE HIS **RIGHT ARM** FOR SCOTLAND! AND HIS LEFT ARM, AND HIS RIGHT LEG, AND... WELL, YOU'LL SEE...

PLEASE GIVE A **BIG HAND** TO SCOTLAND'S BRAVE-HEARTED HERO...

WILLIAM WALLACE!

WILLIAM WALLACE
GUARDIAN OF SCOTLAND
1270–1305

WALLACE, YOU'RE A GREAT HERO TO THE SCOTS FOR DOING WHAT THEY LOVE BEST: **BEATING THE ENGLISH!** BUT WHY WERE YOU FIGHTING THEM AT ALL?

OCHT. SCOTLAND WAS IN A BAD WAY, EVEN **BEFORE** THE ENGLISH ARRIVED...

FIRST, THE KING FELL OFF A CLIFF, RIDING TO A **HOT DATE** WITH HIS NEW WIFE.

NOOOOO OOOO...

NEEEEEIIH

HE HAD NO CHILDREN, SO THE NEXT IN LINE WAS HIS THREE-YEAR-OLD GRANDDAUGHTER, BUT SHE WAS **DROWNED AT SEA.**

GLUG GLUG...

THE SCOTTISH BARONS STARTED A TUG-OF-WAR OVER WHO SHOULD BE KING...

MY GREAT GRAND-UNCLE'S COUSIN WAS KING!

WELL, MY GRANDMOTHER'S FRIEND'S BROTHER WAS KING!

WELL, MY AUNTIE'S CAT'S...

A **CIVIL WAR** WOULD TEAR THE COUNTRY APART! SO SOMEONE HAD A BRIGHT IDEA...

HOLD IT CHAPS! LET'S ASK THE ENGLISH KING, **EDWARD I,** TO DECIDE!

OOH, **THAT'S A GOOD IDEA!**

NOPE. **BAD IDEA!** EDWARD CHOSE THE WEAKEST, RUBBISHEST GUY HE COULD FIND...

I CHOOSE **THIS** GUY. I'M **SURE** HE'LL MAKE A GREAT PUPPET — I MEAN, **KING!**

DUUUUR...

SO **HE** COULD CONTROL HIM!

HEY, GUYS! I'VE GOT A GREAT IDEA — LET'S GIVE EDWARD ALL OUR MONEY!

HUH?!

AW WHAT!?

THEN EDWARD SENT IN HIS ARMY, GOT RID OF THE PUPPET AND MADE **HIMSELF** KING INSTEAD.

WAAA AAH!

HEH HEH.

WELL, I WASN'T GOING TO STAND FOR **THAT!** WE WANTED OUR **OWN** KING, EVEN IF HE **WAS** RUBBISH!

SO I STARTED AN **UPRISING!** A RAG-TAG BAND OF REBELS WITH ONLY ONE GOAL — TO CHASE OUT THE ENGLISH!

BEFORE LONG, YOU WERE EDWARD'S **PUBLIC ENEMY #1!**

WALLACE STOLE ALL MY TAXES!

WALLACE KILLED ALL MY SOLDIERS!

WALLACE **CHOPPED ME IN HALF!**

THIS GUY IS DOING MY **NUT**! SOMEONE GET UP THERE AND **TAKE OUT THIS WALLACE**!

SO EDWARD SENT A HUGE ARMY TO **KILL** YOU AND **SUBDUE** SCOTLAND!

BUT FIRST HE HAD TO **FIND** ME! MY SMALLER, LIGHTER ARMY MEANT I COULD WATCH AND WAIT UNTIL THE PERFECT OPPORTUNITY TO ATACK.

AND THAT OPPORTUNITY CAME WHEN THEY TRIED TO CROSS OVER **STIRLING BRIDGE**...

THE ENGLISH ARMY WAS BIGGER AND BETTER EQUIPPED, BUT I HAD A PLAN TO TURN THAT AGAINST THEM.

I WAITED UNTIL MOST OF THEM HAD CROSSED THE BRIDGE...

...AND THEN WE ATTACKED!

THE SCOTS!

GET THEM!

GET IN LINE!

GET OUT OF MY WAY!

AAAAAAAAAAH!

HILL

BRIDGE

MARSHY GROUND

THEIR HEAVILY ARMOURED KNIGHTS GOT STUCK IN THE SWAMP, AND THE SCOTS PICKED THEM OFF WITH EXTRA-LONG SPEARS.

THE ENGLISH TRIED TO RETREAT ACROSS THE BRIDGE, WHILE THEIR REINFORCEMENTS TRIED TO CHARGE. IT WAS **MAYHEM**!

ATTACK!

RETREAT!

GET OFF MY FOOT!

THE BRIDGE **COLLAPSED** UNDER ALL THEIR WEIGHT, AND THEIR HEAVY ARMOUR PULLED THEM DOWN AND **DROWNED** THEM!

WE WERE ESPECIALLY PLEASED TO HAVE KILLED A GUY CALLED **HUGH DE CRESSINGHAM**. HE WAS IN CHARGE OF STEALING ALL THE SCOTS' **MONEY**.

THE **ROTTER**!

WE **SKINNED** HIM AND EVERY SOLDIER GOT A PIECE!

ONE FOR YOU... ONE FOR YOU...

CAN I GET AN EXTRA PIECE? IT'S FOR MY DAUGHTER...

YOU WERE KNIGHTED AND NAMED "**HIGH GUARDIAN OF SCOTLAND**". YOU WERE RIDING HIGH!

UNTIL I GOT CAPTURED...

I WAS PUT IN TRIAL AS A TRAITOR, BUT I SAID HOW COULD **I** BE A TRAITOR TO EDWARD WHEN HE WAS NEVER MY TRUE KING?

I WAS SENTENCED TO BE **HANGED, DRAWN AND QUARTERED**! IT WAS THE MOST TORTUROUS MODE OF EXECUTION THEY HAD!

FIRST THEY **HANGED** ME UNTIL I WAS ALMOST, BUT NOT QUITE, DEAD...

THEN THEY CUT OPEN MY STOMACH, **DREW** OUT MY **GUTS**, AND SET THEM IN FIRE.

AND THEN THEY CUT OFF MY HEAD.

AND CUT YOU INTO **QUARTERS**!

AND CUT ME INTO QUARTERS...

THUMP!

PULL YOURSELF TOGETHER, MAN!

NOW, LET'S MEET THE MAN WHO LED A **DECADE OF DEFIANCE** AGAINST THE MIGHT OF ENGLAND. TO THE **WELSH** HE'S LIKE KING ARTHUR, ROBIN HOOD AND WILLIAM WALLACE, ALL ROLLED INTO ONE!

PLEASE WELCOME THE LAST WELSHMAN TO **EVER** HOLD THE TITLE **PRINCE OF WALES**, IT'S...

OWAIN GLYNDWR*!

OWAIN GLYNDWR
PRINCE OF WALES
1359–1415

OWAIN, FOR A WELSH FREEDOM FIGHTER, YOU WERE REMARKABLY PALLY WITH THE ENGLISH. YOU WERE **RAISED** BY AN ENGLISH LORD, **MARRIED** HIS DAUGHTER, AND EVEN FOUGHT **IN THEIR ARMY!**

YEAH, I WAS ALWAYS COOL WITH THE ENGLISH. I MEAN, OK, THEY'D INVADED US AND KEPT US OPPRESSED BY BRUTAL FORCE, PUNISHING TAXATION AND UNFAIR LAWS...

BUT THEY'D NEVER DONE ME ANY HARM...

UNTIL, THAT IS, A **NEW** KING CAME TO THE THRONE, THE DASTARDLY...

DUN DUN DAA...

*THE STANDARD ENGLISH VERSION OF OWAIN'S NAME IS **OWEN GLENDOWER.** FOR EXTRA CREDIT YOU CAN TRY THE WELSH PRONUNCIATION, WHICH IS SOMETHING LIKE O-**WINE** GLIN-**DOO**-IR.

HENRY IV!

BOO!

OI! WATCH IT...

AS A LORD, I WAS REQUIRED BY LAW TO GO AND FIGHT FOR THE KING WHEREVER AND WHENEVER HE REQUIRED.

BUT MY NEIGHBOUR, WHO WAS ANOTHER ENGLISH DASTARD, DIDN'T PASS ON THE SUMMONS, SO I GOT BRANDED AN OUTLAW.

BUT, BUT...

NO EXCUSES.

IMAGINE! ME, THE DESCENDANT OF **THREE** OF THE PRINCELY HOUSES OF WALES, HIDING IN THE HILLS LIKE A COMMON BANDIT!

BUT THAT WAS JUST THE SORT OF RUBBISH UNFAIRNESS PEOPLE ALL **OVER** WALES WERE EXPERIENCING, AND THEY WERE GETTING HEARTILY **SICK** OF IT!

A GROUP OF DIE-HARD DESPERADOES JOINED ME, AND TOGETHER WE SNUCK INTO THE FORTIFIED TOWN OF **RUTHIN**.

THEN WE THREW OFF OUR DISGUISES, SLAUGHTERED THE ENGLISH GARRISON, AND BURNED THE PLACE TO THE GROUND!

WELL, AFTER A FEW ATTACKS LIKE THAT, HENRY HAD NO **CHOICE** BUT TO SEND IN AN ARMY TO CAPTURE YOU.

PFF! GOOD **LUCK!** I WAS IN MY **OWN** COUNTRY, SURROUNDED BY FRIENDS, AND WITH A TINY FORCE OF GUERRILLAS. HE COULDN'T EVEN **FIND** ME!

PLUS, THE WEATHER GOT **SO TERRIBLE**, HE HAD TO TURN BACK.

OK. FINE.

PEOPLE STARTED SAYING I WAS A **MAGICIAN**, WHO COULD EVEN CONTROL THE WEATHER!

THEY'VE GONE. YOU CAN TURN IT OFF NOW.

WHEN HE COULDN'T FIND ME, HENRY TOOK IT OUT ON THE WELSH PEOPLE, WITH MASSACRES AND EVEN-MORE BRUTAL TAXES.

BUT THAT JUST MADE THEM **MORE** DETERMINED. NOW MEN FLOCKED TO THE CAUSE OF A FREE WELSH KINGDOM, WHERE THEY WOULD BE OPPRESSED ONLY BY OTHER WELSHMEN.

VERY NOBLE. BUT ENGLAND WAS **SO** MUCH BIGGER THAN WALES, AND THEIR ARMIES WERE SO MUCH BIGGER, TOO! HOW COULD YOU HOPE TO SUCCEED?

WELL, FIRSTLY WITH SUPERIOR TACTICS. LIKE AT ONE BATTLE, I'D BRIBED THE ENEMY ARCHERS, SO IN THE MIDDLE OF THE BATTLE, THEY SUDDENLY CAME OVER TO OUR SIDE!

I CAPTURED THE LEADER OF THAT ARMY, A TOP ENGLISH KNIGHT NAMED **SIR EDMUND MORTIMER**.

UNHAND ME, VARLETS!

NORMAL PROCEDURE WAS TO **RANSOM** IMPORTANT CAPTIVES, BUT HENRY WOULDN'T PAY! TURNS OUT HE THOUGHT MORTIMER WAS AFTER HIS THRONE.

WELL, IF HE WASN'T BEFORE, HE WAS NOW! TEAMING UP WITH HENRY'S ENEMIES WAS ANOTHER OF MY GIANT-KILLING STRATEGIES.

I RE-ESTABLISHED WELSH LAWS, HELD A WELSH PARLIAMENT AND WAS CROWNED PRINCE OF WALES. IT WAS A GOLDEN AGE...

BUT IT'S NOT A HAPPY-ENDING STORY, IS IT, OWAIN?

WELL, TIME WAS NOT ON OUR SIDE. AS THE WAR DRAGGED ON, EVERYONE WAS GETTING MORE AND MORE SICK OF IT.

THE ORDINARY PEOPLE WERE FED UP OF SOLDIERS, ENGLISH **AND** WELSH, EATING THEIR FOOD AND DYING ON THEIR DOORSTEPS.

PLUS, HENRY HAD THE BRIGHT IDEA OF OFFERING **PARDONS** TO EVERYONE WHO HAD FOUGHT AGAINST HIM.

SUDDENLY, GIVING THE WHOLE THING UP AND GOING HOME STARTED TO LOOK **VERY** TEMPTING TO **LOTS** OF MY GUYS...

I HAD TO DO SOMETHING, AND **QUICK!** I TEAMED UP WITH THE **FRENCH** (THOSE GUYS HATED THE ENGLISH EVEN WORSE THAN WE DID) AND TOGETHER **WE** INVADED **THEM!**

ENGLAND — WALES

HENRY **HAD** TO COME AND FIGHT. OUR TWO **MASSIVE** ARMIES FACED OFF ACROSS A DEEP VALLEY.

GRR! GRR!

WHICH WAS KIND OF A PROBLEM. IF **WE** ATTACKED **THEM**, WE'D HAVE TO GO DOWN INTO THE VALLEY, WHERE WE'D GET **SLAUGHTERED**.

AIEE!
ARGH!
OH GOD! THE PAIN!

BUT IF **THEY** ATTACKED **US**, WE'D DO THE SAME. NO ONE WANTED TO MAKE THE FIRST MOVE!

FOR **8 DAYS** WE CAMPED ON THAT HILL, WITH NOTHING TO DO BUT SHARPEN OUR WEAPONS AND WAIT.

I THINK I OVERDID IT...

UNTIL, IN THE END, WE WERE TOO TIRED AND HUNGRY TO FIGHT. HENRY DIDN'T EVEN BOTHER, HE JUST WALKED OFF.

PFF. LATER, LOSERS.

I WANDERED THE HILLS FOR A WHILE, BUT THE HEART HAD GONE OUT OF THE WELSH FIGHT.

AND SO YOUR GREAT CAMPAIGN ENDED, NOT WITH A BANG, BUT WITH A WHIMPER.

NO NEED TO RUB IT IN...

GUERRILLAS IN OUR MIDST

GUERRILLA WARFARE IS THE STRATEGY MOST COMMONLY USED BY MODERN-DAY REBELS FIGHTING AGAINST A LARGER FORCE.

THE WORD WAS FIRST USED BY SPANISH INSURGENTS FIGHTING AGAINST NAPOLEON (IT JUST MEANS "LITTLE WAR" IN SPANISH).

BUT WELSH REBEL LEADER OWAIN GLYNDWR WAS AHEAD OF HIS TIME, USING PROTO-GUERRILLA TACTICS IN HIS WAR AGAINST ENGLISH OCCUPIER HENRY IV HUNDREDS OF YEARS EARLIER!

ALL RIGHT! SO HERE'S OWAIN'S GUERRILLA GUIDELINES, GUARANTEED TO TURN EVEN THE RUNTY-EST REBELLION INTO AN ASYMMETRICAL-WARFARE KING KONG!!

Avoid big battles.

With a smaller army, you'll probably lose.

The only exception to this is if you have some sneaky tricks planned.

Like, I don't know, archers hiding in the trees or something...

Keep on the move.

Less armour and fewer soldiers means you can travel faster.

Hit the enemy when they're not looking, then just melt into the hills.

Win over the people with clever propaganda.

Like, get your bards to sing songs comparing you to the legendary King Arthur, another guy who battled the invading Saxon hordes.

You could also try reducing taxes, championing justice, respecting local traditions...

Basically, what are the enemy doing that everyone's sick of? Do the opposite!

Cause problems.

Burn farms and loot towns still loyal to the enemy.

You've got no chance against a castle, but all this aggravation will hopefully force the enemy to come out looking for you. Then you can pounce!

This also helps with the propaganda since it shows those locals their lords are useless and can't protect them.

Blend in with the local population.

Either you'll escape detection, which is pretty sweet when it happens, let me tell you...

Or else the enemy will attack some innocent bystanders while hunting for you, further turning the population against them.

Target enemy supplies.

Invaders generally need to ship in money, weapons and food from far away.

Find out when their shipments are arriving, and ambush them!

You're supplying your own men and depriving the enemy at the same time. Bonus!

AND LAST, BUT NOT LEAST, **NEVER GIVE UP!** THE CAUSE IS **NOT DEAD** SO LONG AS EVEN ONE **TRUE BELIEVER** YET LIVES!

NOT YOURS THOUGH.

OK, SURE. THE POINT STILL STANDS...

SOME OF THE GREATEST REVOLUTIONS IN HISTORY LOOKED DOOMED FOR **YEARS**, BUT THEY CLUNG ON, LIVED TO FIGHT ANOTHER DAY, AND EVENTUALLY **SUCCEEDED!**

NOW, LET'S MEET THE **RELUCTANT REBEL** WHO HOLDS THE RECORD FOR THE **SHORTEST** REIGN OF **ANY** ENGLISH SOVEREIGN.

IT'S THE MOMENTARY MONARCH, THE FLASH IN A SASH, THE TIME-TRIAL TUDOR, THE **9-DAY** QUEEN...

JANE GREY!

JANE GREY
ENGLISH QUEEN
1537–1554

JANE, YOU MIGHT ALSO BE ENGLAND'S MOST **RELUCTANT** MONARCH — YOU HAD NO DESIRE **WHATSOEVER** TO BECOME QUEEN!

GOD NO!

WHEN THEY SPRUNG IT ON ME, I WAS SO FREAKED OUT I BURST INTO TEARS!

YOU MEAN YOU DIDN'T EVEN **KNOW** YOU WERE BEING MADE QUEEN?

TOTALLY BLINDSIDED ME!

I DIDN'T EVEN KNOW THE KING WAS **DEAD**! AND EVEN THEN, I'D HAVE ASSUMED ONE OF HIS **SISTERS** WOULD GET IT...

OK, WHOA, WHOA. BACK UP A MINUTE. WHAT KING IS THIS?

YEAH, I'M SORRY – IT'S A BIT COMPLICATED...

THE WHOLE MESS IS THANKS TO MY GRAND-UNCLE **HENRY VIII**, COS HE DIVORCED HIS FIRST WIFE AND BEHEADED HIS SECOND.

HEYY!

WIFE NUMBER **3** ↝

THE KING **I** KNEW WAS HIS SON, **EDWARD VI**, BUT HE DIED YOUNG AND CHILDLESS.

AW WHAT!?

RELAX... **WE'RE** BOTH DEAD ALREADY...

EDWARD

HENRY ALSO HAD TWO **DAUGHTERS**, BUT KING EDWARD HAD SPECIFICALLY BANNED THEM FROM BECOMING QUEEN BECAUSE OF THE WHOLE DIVORCE/BEHEADING THING.

HEY, **NICE** ONE, BRO!

MARY   ELIZABETH

ALSO MARY WAS A CATHOLIC, SO **EVERYONE** WANTED TO KEEP **HER** OFF THE THRONE. WHICH JUST LEFT **ME**...

GRR...   WATCH IT, YOU!

BUT NO ONE EXPECTED EDWARD TO DIE, SO NO ONE EXPECTED ME TO HAVE **ANY** CHANCE AT THE THRONE.

YUP, I WAS JUST PLAIN OL' **LADY JANE** FOR MOST OF MY LIFE.

BUT THAT WAS NEVER ENOUGH FOR YOUR PARENTS...

GOD, WHAT A **NIGHTMARE**! ALL THEY EVER THOUGHT ABOUT WAS GETTING ME MARRIED TO SOME RICH LORD!

NO MATTER WHAT I WAS DOING, IT WAS NEVER GOOD ENOUGH FOR THEM.

JANE! WRONG KNIFE!

JANE! SIT UP STRAIGHT!

JANE! DON'T BREATHE!

GOOD GRIEF! NO ONE WILL **EVER** WANT TO MARRY YOU!

GEEZ. SOUNDS PRETTY ROUGH.

YEAH – ALL I EVER REALLY WANTED WAS TO BE LEFT ALONE WITH MY READING.

45

Panel 1:
IT WAS MY ONE REFUGE. BUT EVEN **THAT** DIDN'T LAST...

JANE!

GOOD NEWS...

Panel 2:
WE'VE ARRANGED FOR YOU TO MARRY **LORD GUILFORD DUDLEY!**

HIS DADDY'S THE RICHEST LORD IN ENGLAND!

Panel 3:
I WAS SO **MISERABLE!** I DIDN'T **LOVE** DUDLEY. I DIDN'T EVEN **KNOW** HIM!

Panel 4:
THEN ONE DAY I WAS SUMMONED TO COURT...

UH. HEY GUYS. WHAT'S GOING ON?

...OH.

Panel 5:
I **BEGGED** THEM TO JUST LEAVE ME ALONE, BUT THEY INSISTED KING EDWARD HAD CHOSEN **ME** TO BE **QUEEN** BEFORE HE DIED, AND I HAD TO ACCEPT IT.

Panel 6:
BUT THEN...

SO... UH... NOW YOU'RE QUEEN... I GET TO BE KING, RIGHT?

HUSBAND, DUDLEY JR.

Panel 7:
SUDDENLY, THE PENNY DROPPED! IT WAS ALL A **SET-UP!**

Panel 8:
REMEMBER **DUDLEY** SR. WAS THE RICHEST AND MOST POWERFUL LORD IN ENGLAND...

Panel 9:
HE KNEW THE KING WAS DYING, SO HE'D ARRANGED MY MARRIAGE, **AND** GOT THE KING TO NOMINATE ME...

JANE? GOOD IDEA. AT LEAST SHE'S NOT A **CATHOLIC.**

THAT'S RIGHT, YOUR MAJESTY.

Panel 10:
ALL SO HIS DUMMY OF A SON COULD BECOME **KING!**

NO **WAY.** YOU CAN BE A **DUKE** IF YOU LIKE.

WAAAH!

I'M TELLING MUMMY!

Panel 11:
BUT HE REALLY HAD SOMETHING TO CRY ABOUT SOON ENOUGH! TURNS OUT THE PEOPLE DIDN'T **WANT** SOME GIRL THEY'D NEVER HEARD OF AS QUEEN...

Panel 12:
THEY DIDN'T CARE ABOUT SOME ABSTRACT LEGITIMACY DISPUTE!

WHO IS THIS GREY GIRL?

MARY IS HENRY'S DAUGHTER. MAKE **HER** QUEEN!

MARY CAME MARCHING IN WITH A HUGE ARMY OF SUPPORTERS AND **BOOM!** MY **9-DAY** REIGN WAS OVER.

YOU KNOW, YOU MIGHT HAVE ACHIEVED **LESS** THAN ANYONE I'VE EVER HAD ON THIS SHOW...

GIVE ME A BREAK! I'D LIKE TO SEE HOW **YOU'D** HAVE DONE, AGED **16**, AGAINST THE MOST POWERFUL PEOPLE IN THE COUNTRY!

I WAS MADE A PRISONER IN THE TOWER OF LONDON.

BRUTAL.

IT WAS ACTUALLY PRETTY NICE.

I WASN'T IN A CELL OR ANYTHING... I HAD NICE ROOMS, I COULD READ IN THE GARDENS, AND I WASN'T BOTHERED BY MY HUSBAND OR HIS AWFUL FAMILY (THEY WERE TOO BUSY GETTING EXECUTED).

OOH HOO HOO HO...

CHOP!

IN FACT, IF IT WASN'T FOR ALL THE **BEHEADING**, IT WOULD'VE BEEN THE HAPPIEST TIME OF MY LIFE.

BUT IT WASN'T LONG BEFORE IT WAS **YOUR** TURN...

EVEN THOUGH I NEVER EVEN **WANTED** THE CROWN, QUEEN MARY DECIDED I WAS TOO MUCH OF A **THREAT.**

I'M SORRY M'LADY

I FORGIVE YOU, EXECUTIONER. JUST MAKE IT QUICK.

I TRIED **REALLY HARD** TO ACT COOL, BUT WHEN I COULDN'T FIND THE EXECUTION BLOCK, I STARTED TO PANIC.

AH! WHERE IS IT!?

I GUESS YOU MIGHT SAY THAT YOU **LOST YOUR HEAD**...?

YOU'VE MADE THAT JOKE BEFORE, HAVEN'T YOU?

47

*ROUGHLY: GRAW-NYEH NEE WAW-YEH. (OR, IF YOU'RE NOT BRAVE ENOUGH TO TACKLE ALL THOSE GAELIC VOWELS, GRACE O'MALLEY)

50

AFTER THAT **CLOSE SHAVE**, HE HAD TO TAKE ME!

YOUR COURAGE AND SKILL SOON MADE YOU A FAVOURITE WITH THE SAILORS.

AND MY HABIT OF SAVING THEIR LIVES! ONE TIME WE WERE UNDER ATTACK FROM PIRATES, AND GETTING THE WORST OF IT...

UNTIL I PULLED OFF A CRUSHING DEATH-FROM-ABOVE **ELBOW SMASH** OFF THE TOP RIGGING, TURNING THE BATTLE.

BUT YOUR **HAIR-RAISING** ADVENTURES ALMOST CAME TO AN END WHEN YOU WERE MARRIED OFF TO THE SON OF ANOTHER LOCAL CLAN: DONAL "SON OF BATTLE" O'FLAHERTY.

THAT'S JUST HOW IT WORKED BACK THEN. THE O'FLAHERTYS HAD MORE LAND, MORE SHIPS, MORE CASTLES, SO IT WAS A STEP UP FOR OUR LITTLE CLAN.

BUT DONAL "SON OF BATTLE" LIVED UP TO HIS NAME - HE WAS ALWAYS OFF PICKING FIGHTS. SO **I** ENDED UP RUNNING THE O'FLAHERTY CLAN LANDS, SHIPS **AND** CASTLES.

IN THE END HE PICKED A FIGHT WITH THE WRONG NEIGHBOURS AND GOT HIMSELF KILLED.

I AVENGED HIM, OF COURSE, BUT HIS CLAN COULDN'T HANDLE A WOMAN RUNNING THE SHOW, SO THEY KICKED ME OUT! AFTER **19** YEARS OF DEDICATED SERVICE TOO...

SO WITH NOTHING BUT A FEW LOYAL FOLLOWERS, AND SOME ROCK-SOLID ADMIN EXPERIENCE, YOU RETURNED TO YOUR OLD CASTLE, BECOMING QUEEN OF A TINY STRIP OF ATLANTIC COAST.

YEAH, NOT FOR LONG THOUGH... I IMMEDIATELY SET TO WORK BUILDING THAT TINY KINGDOM INTO A MIGHTY PIRATE EMPIRE.

FIRST I SUPPLEMENTED MY MEAGRE FORCES WITH **GALLOWGLASS** MERCENARIES FROM SCOTLAND, BASICALLY A TERRIFYING CROSS BETWEEN HIGHLANDERS AND VIKINGS.

BACKED BY THESE CLAYMORE-WIELDING COERCION-ARTISTS, I STARTED COLLECTING TOLLS FROM WHOEVER WANTED TO SAIL THROUGH OUR WATERS.

AND IF THEY DIDN'T WANT TO PAY, WELL, OK. WE'D JUST TAKE IT THE HARD WAY...

AS YOUR EMPIRE EXPANDED, YOUR NEWLY WON PIRATE QUEEN STATUS COMMANDED AN APPROPRIATE DEGREE OF **RESPECT**.

AND I EXPECTED TO GET IT!

ONE TIME I STOPPED BY A LOCAL EARL'S CASTLE FOR SOME DINNER, BUT HE REFUSED TO LET ME IN!

ER, SORRY. WE'RE, UM, NOT HERE...?

THAT'S A TERRIBLE INSULT TO A PROUD IRISH QUEEN!

SO I KIDNAPPED HIS SON UNTIL HE APOLOGISED AND AGREED TO FEED ME **WHENEVER** I WANTED.

LITERALLY, HE HAD TO HAVE AN **EXTRA PLACE** SET FOR ME AT ALL MEALS, IN CASE I HAPPENED TO DROP BY.

JUST CHECKING...

YOU ALSO FOUND TIME TO GET MARRIED TO ANOTHER LOCAL LORD, THOUGH HE DIDN'T LAST TOO LONG.

WELL, IRISH LAW LET COUPLES TEST-DRIVE A MARRIAGE FOR A YEAR - THEY CALLED IT THE "ONE YEAR CERTAIN" SYSTEM'.

BUT AFTER A YEAR, I WAS **CERTAIN** I DIDN'T WANT HIM. SO I JUST CHANGED ALL THE LOCKS ON HIS CASTLE, CHUCKED HIS STUFF IN THE MOAT AND DUMPED HIM FROM THE BATTLEMENTS!

HE DID GIVE ME A SON, THOUGH, WHO WAS BORN AT SEA DURING A PARTICULARLY FEROCIOUS ATTACK BY RIVAL PIRATES.

MY GUYS WERE LOSING SO I HAD TO RUN OUT AND FIGHT THEM OFF MYSELF.

DO I HAVE TO DO **EVERYTHING** AROUND HERE?!

EVENTUALLY, YOUR PIRATICAL ANTICS BECAME TOO MUCH FOR THE ENGLISH GOVERNOR.

PIRATE QUEEN, EH WHAT? CAN'T BALLY WELL HAVE THAT...

HEY LOOK, PIRATING YOUR NEIGHBOURS WAS BASICALLY AN UNAVOIDABLE WAY OF LIFE BACK THEN. HIS **REAL** ISSUE WAS BECAUSE I REFUSED TO SUBMIT TO ENGLISH RULE!

AT THIS TIME, THE ENGLISH QUEEN **ELIZABETH I** WAS TRYING TO FORCE ALL THE IRISH CHIEFTAINS TO ACCEPT HER AS THEIR OVERLORD.

THOSE WHO AGREED HAD TO GIVE UP THEIR TRADITIONAL CUSTOMS: LANGUAGE, LAWS, CLOTHES, EVEN RELIGION.

THOSE WHO RESISTED GOT, WELL, WHAT I GOT. MY LANDS WERE BURNED, MY SHIPS CONFISCATED AND MY PORTS CLOSED.

I FOUGHT BACK WITH EVERYTHING I HAD, BUT THEN THEY WENT FOR MY FAMILY. MY ELDEST SON GOT TRICKED AND EXECUTED, MY MIDDLE SON BETRAYED **ME** AND SIDED WITH THE ENGLISH...

OOH, I WAS SO MAD! I INVADED HIS LANDS, THE UNGRATEFUL WRETCH, BURNED HIS FIELDS, AND REFUSED TO SPEAK TO HIM EVER AGAIN.

WHICH MADE **CHRISTMAS** AKWARD...

TELL MY **SO-CALLED** SON TO PASS THE GRAVY. OR I'LL SET HIS SPROUTS ALIGHT.

MUUUM!

BUT WHEN MY YOUNGEST SON WAS IMPRISONED, I HAD ONLY ONE OPTION LEFT. I SAILED TO LONDON TO PUT MY CASE TO ELIZABETH, QUEEN TO QUEEN.

OK, IT DIDN'T GET OFF TO A GREAT START, AFTER THEY FOUND MY **HIDDEN DAGGER**, BUT I EXPLAINED THAT'S JUST WHAT **ALL** PIRATE QUEENS CARRY IN THEIR UNDERWEAR.

ALSO I REFUSED TO BOW TO HER, SINCE WE WERE BOTH QUEENS. **AND** SHE HAD TO DO THE WHOLE MEETING IN LATIN SINCE THERE WAS NO WAY I WAS GOING TO SPEAK **ENGLISH**.

THINKING ABOUT IT, IT'S A MIRACLE SHE DIDN'T HAVE ME **EXECUTED**...

BUT INSTEAD SHE AGREED TO RELEASE MY SON AND FIRE THAT IDIOT GOVERNOR.

AND I WAS ABLE TO CARRY ON PIRATING, SO LONG AS I ONLY PIRATED HER ENEMIES.

WOW. YOU MUST'VE REALLY DRIVEN AN **ARR'D** BARGAIN!

RIGHT?

BECAUSE PIRATES SAY...

OK, OK! I GET IT!

OUR NEXT **INCENDIARY INSURGENT** IS BRITAIN'S FAVOURITE **PARLIAMENTARY PYROMANIAC!**

PLEASE GIVE AN **EXPLOSIVE** WELCOME TO THE MAN WITH THE **DYNAMITE** PLAN...

GUY FAWKES!

GUY FAWKES
CONSPIRATOR
1570–1606

GUY, YOUR **TOTAL FAILURE** TO BLOW UP PARLIAMENT ON NOVEMBER 5TH, **1605** IS STILL CELEBRATED EACH YEAR WITH BONFIRES AND FIREWORKS.

HOW DOES IT FEEL TO BE COMMEMORATED AS HISTORY'S MOST **PATHETIC, UNMITIGATED BUNGLER?**

VERILY, THAT'S A BIT HARSH!

OK, IT DIDN'T WORK OUT, BUT IT WAS A GOOD PLAN! WE JUST HAD A STROKE OF BAD LUCK...

THERE'S NO SUCH THING AS BAD LUCK, ONLY **POOR PREPARATIONS**. AND I PUT IT TO YOU THAT YOUR "PLOT" WAS THE MOST POORLY PREPARED, SHODDY, AMATEUR DOG'S BREAKFAST OF A PLAN IMAGINABLE!

WAS NOT!

WAS TOO!

WAS NOT!

OK, LET'S JUST TELL THE STORY, AND LET THE READERS DECIDE...

WELL, IT WAS A WILD AND STORMY NIGHT WHEN WE HELD OUR FIRST, FATEFUL MEETING...

FIVE DESPERADOES, HAND-PICKED FOR DARING, EXPERTISE, AND PASSIONATE COMMITMENT TO OUR CAUSE...

CATESBY "THE BRAINS"

WRIGHT "THE MUSCLE"

PERCY "THE MONEY"

FAWKES "DEMOLITION"

WINTOUR "THE WHEELMAN"

NOW, YOU ALL KNOW WHY WE ARE HERE... JING JAMES HAS PERSECUTED THE FOLLOWERS OF THE TRUE CATHOLIC FAITH FOR LONG ENOUGH!

BOO!

YAY!

SOMETHING MUST BE DONE. SOMETHING **EXPLODE-Y**! MAY I INTRODUCE OUR VERY OWN MR DYNAMITE...

GUY FAWKES!

GENTLEMEN...

LET ME ASK YOU ONE QUESTION! WHEN ARE THE KING AND HIS PARLIAMENT ALL IN ONE PLACE AT THE SAME TIME?

BOO!

HISS!

UH...

I DUNNO...

AT THE **OPENING OF PARLIAMENT**!

I WAS JUST ABOUT TO SAY THAT...

OH YEAH...

HERE'S WHAT WE DO... FIRST, WE DIG A TUNNEL FROM PERCY'S HOUSE, **HERE**.

WE BRING IN A SHED-LOAD OF EXPLOSIVES UNDER THE PARLIAMENT BUILDINGS, **HERE**

THEN, WHEN THE KING ARRIVES, IT'S **BOOM-TIME!**

BOO!

THEN, WHILE I'M ESCAPING TO FRANCE, YOU OTHERS START A **REBELLION!**

WE KIDNAP THE KING'S DAUGHTER, THE PRINCESS, AND CROWN HER THE NEW QUEEN.

BOO!

THEN, WE GET HER TO MARRY A CATHOLIC LORD, AND ALL OUR PROBLEMS ARE SOLVED! ANY QUESTIONS?

NONE!

WHAT CAN POSSIBLY GO WRONG!?

PLENTY! LIKE WHAT IF SHE DIDN'T **WANT** TO MARRY A CATHOLIC LORD? ESPECIALLY SINCE YOU GUYS JUST BLEW UP HER DAD!

IT COULD'VE WORKED...

IT **DIDN'T** WORK! YOU DIDN'T EVEN **GET** TO THAT BIT OF YOUR **CRACKPOT SCHEME,** 'COS YOU KEPT **MESSING IT UP!**

FIRST YOU GAVE UP ON THE TUNNEL...

MAN, THIS IS **HARD WORK!**

THERE **HAS** TO BE AN EASIER WAY...

TURNS OUT, THERE WERE ABANDONED CELLARS UNDER THE PARLIAMENT. WE JUST HAD TO RENT ONE OUT. **MUCH** EASIER!

FIREWOOD

GUNPOWDER

THERE! PERFECT!

IN FACT, MAYBE A LITTLE **TOO** EASY, HUH?

AHEM! WELL, **SURE,** EASY TO SAY THAT **NOW...**

THEN THE WHOLE THING HAD TO BE POSTPONED...

THEY DELAYED PARLIAMENT BECAUSE OF THE **PLAGUE!** YOU THINK I SHOULD'VE PLANNED FOR **THAT!?**

A TRUE PROFESSIONAL PREPARES FOR **EVERYTHING...**

AND YOU ALL STARTED GETTING **COLD FEET...**

WELL, WHAT IF WE BLEW UP SOME OF OUR **FRIENDS?** THERE WERE SOME CATHOLIC LORDS GOING TO BE THERE...

SO YOU WROTE TO THEM...

My lord,

I can't say what, but something bad is going to happen. You might want to avoid Parliament for a while...

P.S. please don't show this to the King... (Boo!)

SO **OBVIOUSLY,** THEY SHOWED IT TO THE KING!

BOO!

HIS GUARDS SEARCHED PARLIAMENT, **INCLUDING** THE CELLARS, AND **WHO** DID THEY FIND, SKULKING AROUND WITH A POCKETWATCH, A BOX OF MATCHES AND A LONG FUSE...

YOUR WHOLE GANG WAS CAPTURED, TORTURED AND PUT TO DEATH. THE **GUNPOWDER PLOT** WAS OVER...

AND EVEN WHILE YOU WERE STILL ALIVE, ALL OVER THE COUNTRY PEOPLE WERE LIGHTING BONFIRES TO CELEBRATE.

OH LOOK! FIREWORKS!

AND THE TRADITION CONTINUES TO THIS DAY, REMINDING US ALL OF THE DANGERS OF POOR PLANNING AND THE IMPORTANCE OF BEING PREPARED!

FSSSH! FSSH! FSSH!

SHOULD'VE BEEN PREPARED FOR **THAT**...

GUNPOWDER, TREASON AND PLOT

THE OLD PARLIAMENT BUILDINGS WERE HOUSED IN A JUMBLED MAZE OF PALACES, PASSAGES, PUBS, SHOPS AND PEOPLE'S HOMES THAT MADE UP THE **WESTMINSTER PALACE** COMPLEX.

WE HAD MANAGED TO RENT A HOUSE **RIGHT NEXT** TO THE HOUSE OF LORDS.

EVEN BETTER, IT ALSO GAVE US ACCESS TO THE UNUSED **CELLAR** RIGHT NEXT DOOR!

PLOTTER'S HOUSE

STAIRWAY TO BISHOP'S ENTRANCE

I POSED AS A SERVANT LOYALLY MINDING HIS MASTER'S HOME, BUT **REALLY** I WAS CASING THE JOINT, WATCHING FOR GUARD PATROLS OR SHARP-EYED NEIGHBOURS WHO MIGHT GIVE THE GAME AWAY.

DON'T MIND ME, YER WORSHIP...

PLOT MASTERMIND **ROBERT CATESBY** OWNED A HOUSE JUST ACROSS THE RIVER THAMES.

PASSAGEWAY TO CELLAR

WE STORED THE GUNPOWDER THERE AND THEN FERRIED IT ACROSS, BARREL BY BARREL, UNDER COVER OF NIGHT.

PASSAGEWAY TO RIVER

ALL OF THIS ACTUALLY BEARS LITTLE RESEMBLANCE TO THE **CURRENT** PARLIAMENT BUILDINGS ON THE SAME SITE.

IT HAD TO BE REBUILT AFTER THE WHOLE THING WAS **BURNED DOWN** BY ACCIDENT.

BAH! I SHOULD'VE JUST WAITED...

NOW FOR ONE OF THE MOST **CONTROVERSIAL** REBELS IN ENGLISH HISTORY! WAS HE AN INSANE DICTATOR, DRUNK WITH POWER, OR THE FOUNDER OF MODERN DEMOCRACY? OR **BOTH!**

GET READY FOR A **WARTS-AND-ALL** LOOK AT...

OLIVER CROMWELL!

OLIVER CROMWELL
MILITARY DICTATOR
1599–1658

CROMWELL, YOU ARE REMEMBERED AS THE MOST IMPORTANT FIGURE OF THE **ENGLISH CIVIL WAR.** WHAT WAS ALL THE FIGHTING ABOUT?

THE FIGHTING WAS BECAUSE KING CHARLES I WAS A TOTAL **POO-HEAD!**

CORPSE TALK: ALWAYS A BALANCED VIEW...

OH, COME ON! HE WAS ALWAYS ABUSING HIS POWER, MAKING UP NEW LAWS AND TAXES JUST SO HE COULD GET RICH.

WELL, I'M THE **KING**! I CAN DO WHAT I LIKE! AFTER ALL, I WAS APPOINTED BY **GOD**.

NO, YOU WERE APPOINTED TO SERVE **GOD'S PEOPLE**. YOU HAVE TO GET **PARLIAMENT'S** PERMISSION FOR ALL THESE TAXES...

OH PIFFLE!

I'LL GET MY ARMY, AND WE'LL SHOW **YOU**!

OH YEAH! WELL, MY ARMY'S **WAY** BETTER THAN YOURS!

THE KING'S SUPPORTERS, ALSO CALLED THE **CAVALIERS**, WERE LAZY AND POORLY DISCIPLINED.

A BATTLE? OK, HOLD ON. I'LL BE RIGHT THERE...

BUT **MY** GUYS (CALLED **ROUNDHEADS** BECAUSE OF THEIR SHORT HAIRSTYLES) WERE DISCIPLINED, HIGHLY TRAINED AND PUMPED UP ON THE **WORD OF GOD**!

WOO!

I RECRUITED THEM EXCLUSIVELY FROM AMONGST THE **PURITANS** - HARDCORE CHRISTIANS WHO BELIEVED IN A RIGID, MORALLY PURE CHURCH. LIKE ME!

SINCE WE KNEW GOD WAS ON OUR SIDE, WE WENT INTO BATTLE FEARLESSLY AND JOYOUSLY.

WHO **ARE** THESE GUYS!?

ON-WARD ♪ ♪ CHRISTIAN ♪ ♪ SO-O-LDIERS... ♪

WAIT. **GOD** WAS ON **YOUR** SIDE? HOW DID YOU... UM... **KNOW**?

I **WON**! IF GOD **WASN'T** ON MY SIDE, I'D HAVE LOST.

AH! CAN'T ARGUE WITH **THAT**, CAN YOU?

I - UH...

HM.

WE CAPTURED THE KING AND MADE HIM PROMISE TO BEHAVE.

I'M VERY SORRY. I WON'T DO IT AGAIN...

63

BUT HE WAS LYING! RIGHT AWAY HE ESCAPED AND WENT BACK TO WAR AGAIN.

HAD MY FINGERS CROSSED!

MAN, **SERIOUSLY**! HOW DO YOU **REASON** WITH A GUY LIKE THAT!?

SO YOU DECIDED TO KILL HIM.

IT WASN'T JUST **MY** DECISION! HE WAS TRIED AND FOUND GUILTY OF **TREASON**!

RIGHT, BUT **YOUR** ARMY KEPT HIS SUPPORTERS AWAY FROM THE TRIAL.

YES, OK, THAT HELPED. BUT HE **HAD** TO DIE. THE WAR WOULD NEVER HAVE ENDED OTHERWISE.

THEN YOU WENT AFTER HIS **SON**, WHO WAS HIDING OUT IN IRELAND.

NOT HIDING! STARTING ANOTHER WAR!

WELL, YOU SURE PUT A STOP TO THAT! YOU KILLED SO MANY PEOPLE, THE IRISH **STILL** USE YOUR NAME AS A SWEAR WORD!

THEY... WHAT? REALLY!?

YEAH. LIKE "WHAT A TOTAL **CROMWELL**" OR "OH, **CROMWELL**"!

HA! THAT'S PRETTY COOL.

THE IRISH DON'T THINK IT'S COOL! THOSE GUYS **HATE** YOU!

MEH. CAN'T PLEASE EVERYONE.

WELL, YOU DIDN'T PLEASE **ANYONE**!

THAT'S NOT TRUE. I KEPT THE **PURITANS** PRETTY HAPPY...

AND THE ONE THING THAT MADE PURITANS **REALLY** HAPPY WAS STOPPING **EVERYONE ELSE'S** FUN!

YOU GOT RID OF ALL THE OLD **FEAST** DAYS AND INTRODUCED **FAST** DAYS INSTEAD.

OH BOY!

SWEARING WAS ILLEGAL...

OH, **CROMWELL!**

OOP!

AS WAS MAKE-UP. YOU HAD ROAMING SQUADS OF SOLDIERS TO SCRUB THE FACES OF WOMEN CAUGHT WEARING IT!

YOU BANNED DRINKING, COCK-FIGHTING, BEAR-BAITING, GAMBLING, AND GOING TO THE THEATRE...

YOU EVEN BANNED **CHRISTMAS.** COME ON. THAT'S JUST **MEAN!**

LOOK. HAVING FUN WAS AN **EVIL DISTRACTION,** KEEPING PEOPLE FROM WHAT THEY **SHOULD'VE** BEEN DOING.

WHICH WAS...?

READING THE **BIBLE.**

NEEDLESS TO SAY, YOU BECAME **ENORMOUSLY** UNPOPULAR.

CAN'T THINK WHY...

YOU TOOK TO WEARING A **MAIL SHIRT** UNDER YOUR CLOTHES AND SLEEPING IN A DIFFERENT ROOM EVERY NIGHT, IN CASE OF ASSASSINATION ATTEMPTS.

BUT YOU FOILED THEM BY **DYING FIRST!**

HEH! PRETTY TRICKY, HUH?

MY NEXT GUEST MIGHT JUST BE THE MOST MORALLY MINDED **MASS MURDERER** IN THE WHOLE OF HISTORY, AN **INDEFATIGABLE IDEALIST** WHO WENT FROM **RIGHTEOUS REVOLUTIONARY** TO **TYRANNOSAURUS OF TERROR** IN A MATTER OF MONTHS...

PLEASE WELCOME THE **FRENCH REVOLUTION'S DAPPER DECAPITATOR**...

MAXIMILIEN ROBESPIERRE!

MAXIMILIEN ROBESPIERRE

REVOLUTIONARY

1758-1794

ROBESPIERRE, YOU CAME TO POWER IN **THE FRENCH REVOLUTION**: THE REVOLUTION THAT REWROTE THE REVOLUTIONARY RULEBOOK; OVERTHROWING THE OLD ORDER AND PLUNGING FRANCE INTO A NIGHTMARE OF BLOOD AND TERROR.

SO WHAT GOT YOU STARTED ON THE REVOLUTIONARY ROAD?

WELL, REALLY, I JUST WANTED TO HELP PEOPLE.

AND THE POOR PEOPLE OF PRE-REVOLUTIONARY FRANCE NEEDED ALL THE HELP THEY COULD GET!

AN UNFAIR AND FRANKLY UNINTELLIGIBLE MAZE OF ANCIENT LAWS AND RANDOM TAXES ALLOWED A PARASITIC PACK OF **NOBLES** TO BULLY, EXPLOIT AND SWINDLE THE COMMON PEOPLE MERCILESSLY.

I BECAME A LAWYER TO BRING JUSTICE TO THOSE TOO **POOR** AND DOWNTRODDEN TO GET HELP ANYWHERE ELSE.

I COULD'VE BEEN A JUDGE (A MUCH BETTER-PAYING JOB) BUT I COULDN'T FACE HAVING TO SENTENCE PEOPLE TO DEATH.

A BARBARIC PRACTICE – UNFIT FOR A ENLIGHTENED NATION LIKE FRANCE.

AND SO THERE I MIGHT HAVE STAYED, SELFLESSLY TOILING AWAY AS A POOR COUNTRY LAWYER.

IF IT HADN'T BEEN FOR THE **KING**...

THE KING?

LOUIS **XVI**. HE WAS **ALSO** HAVING TROUBLE WITH THE NOBLES, SINCE ONE OF THEIR MAIN PRIVILEGES WAS THAT THEY COULD **COLLECT** ALL THESE TAXES BUT THEY DIDN'T HAVE TO **PAY** ANY TO HIM!

AFTER YEARS OF BAD DECISIONS AND TERRIBLE HARVESTS, THE KING HAD NO MONEY TO RUN THE COUNTRY, AND THE POOR DIDN'T EVEN HAVE MONEY TO BUY FOOD. IT WAS A FULL-ON NATIONAL **DISASTER**.

THE KING TRIED TO PASS NEW LAWS, REQUIRING THE NOBLES TO PAY TAXES TOO, BUT HE NEEDED PARLIAMENT'S APPROVAL. A PARLIAMENT MADE UP OF ALL THESE SAME NOBLES.

SORRY, YOUR MAJ, BUT THAT'S A HARD **NON, MERCI**...

SO HE DECIDED TO TRY CALLING AN **ANCIENT** FORM OF THE PARLIAMENT, ONE THAT HADN'T BEEN USED FOR **CENTURIES**, THAT INCLUDED NOBLES, THE CHURCHMEN, **AND** THE COMMON PEOPLE.

I MANAGED TO GET MYSELF ELECTED AS A REPRESENTATIVE OF THE COMMON PEOPLE. THIS WAS MY CHANCE, NOT JUST TO FIGHT UNFAIR LAWS, BUT TO **CHANGE** THEM.

THE KING'S PLAN WAS TO GET US COMMONERS TO VOTE THROUGH HIS NEW LAWS, DESPITE THE NOBLES' OBJECTIONS.

BRILLIANT! IT CAN'T FAIL...

BUT WHEN WE ALL GOT TOGETHER, WE STARTED TO THINK THAT, YOU KNOW WHAT? **US COMMONERS** WERE BETTER PLACED TO DECIDE WHAT FRANCE NEEDED THAN THE NOBLES **OR** THE KING.

YEAH!

HEAR HEAR!

WE DECLARED **OURSELVES** THE LEGITIMATE GOVERNMENT, WHICH DIDN'T GO DOWN TOO WELL WITH LOUIS.

THEY DID **WHAT**!?

HE SENT IN THE **ARMY** TO TRY AND INTIMIDATE US BACK INTO LINE.

THOSE UNGRATEFUL PEASANTS! I'LL SHOW 'EM...

WHICH DROVE THE POOR PEOPLE OF PARIS **NUTS**! JUST WHEN THEY'D GOT A PARLIAMENT THAT MIGHT ACTUALLY CARE ABOUT **THEM**, IT WAS GOING TO BE DESTROYED.

IT WAS ACTUALLY AN OLD SCHOOL-FRIEND OF MINE, **CAMILLE DESMOULINS**, WHO SPARKED THE PARIS REBELLION.

ARE WE GONNA PUT UP WITH THIS!? I'D RATHER **DIE**!

AN ANGRY MOB FORMED, RANSACKING EVERY BLACKSMITH'S AND WEAPONS SHOP IN THE CITY, EVEN PLUNDERING GUNPOWDER FROM THE **BASTILLE**, THE ANCIENT FORTRESS OF PARIS.

WITH A HEAVILY ARMED REVOLUTIONARY MOB NOW IN CONTROL OF THE CAPITAL, THE KING DECIDED A GOVERNMENT OF COMMONERS WAS A GREAT IDEA AFTER ALL.

NOW IN CONTROL OF THE COUNTRY, THE NEW PARLIAMENT LOST NO TIME ABOLISHING UNJUST LAWS, STRIPPING AWAY UNFAIR ARISTOCRATIC PRIVILEGES AND USHERING IN A NEW ERA OF **FREEDOM**, **EQUALITY** AND **BROTHERHOOD**.

BUT THE GOOD VIBES DIDN'T LAST LONG...

WELL, THERE WAS STILL THE WHOLE PROBLEM OF WHAT TO DO WITH THE KING...

I MEAN, WE **TRIED** TO WORK WITH HIM, AND HE **CLAIMED** HE WAS COMMITTED TO IDEALS OF THE REVOLUTION...

BUT THEN WE CAUGHT HIM TRYING TO SNEAK OFF TO VISIT HIS IN-LAWS, THE **AUSTRIANS**.

THAT SOUNDS... ALL RIGHT..? NICE FAMILY VISIT...

THE **REASON** HE WAS SNEAKING OFF WAS TO BRING IN AN AUSTRIAN **ARMY** TO **SLAUGHTER** HIS OWN PEOPLE AND MAKE HIMSELF AN ABSOLUTE MONARCH AGAIN!

I ARGUED THAT AS LONG AS THE KING WAS ALIVE HE COULD NEVER BE TRUSTED. THERE WOULD **ALWAYS** BE PLOTS TO PUT HIM BACK ON THE THRONE.

AND SO, TO ENSURE THE SAFETY OF THE REVOLUTION, LOUIS **XVI** WAS SENT TO THAT NEWLY INVENTED ENGINE OF ENLIGHTENED EXECUTION, THE **GUILLOTINE**.

UM, WHAT HAPPENED YOU YOUR WHOLE "THE DEATH PENALTY IS BARBARIC" THING?

THAT WAS FOR **REGULAR** CRIMES! A TOTALLY DIFFERENT THING!

TOTALLY.

THE REVOLUTION WAS AN **UNPRECEDENTED** ATTEMPT TO BUILD AN ABSOLUTELY FAIR AND JUST SOCIETY. ANY THREATS TO ITS SUCCESS **HAD** TO BE REMOVED — FOR THE GOOD OF EVERYONE!

AND WE WERE **SURROUNDED** BY THREATS. EXILED NOBLES HAD TEAMED UP WITH BASICALLY **ALL** OF FRANCE'S NEIGHBOURS AND WERE INVADING FROM EVERY DIRECTION, WHILE **MASSIVE** REVOLTS PLUNGED THE COUNTRYSIDE INTO CHAOS.

BUT BY RECRUITING **EVERY** ABLE-BODIED YOUNG MAN IN FRANCE, WE WERE ABLE TO RAISE AN ABSOLUTELY MASSIVE ARMY AND BEAT THEM ALL!

DO IT FOR THE REVOLUTION!

OR GET GUILLOTINED. YOUR CHOICE...

...JUST ONE OF THE MANY **INCREDIBLE** INNOVATIONS OF THE NEWLY FORMED **COMMITTEE OF PUBLIC SAFETY** OF WHICH -AHEM- I WAS A LEADING MEMBER...

COMMITTEE OF PUBLIC SAFETY? SOUNDS KINDA BORING.

AU CONTRAIRE! IT WAS OUR JOB TO DO **WHATEVER IT TOOK** TO KEEP THE PRECIOUS REVOLUTION SAFE.

BUT WHAT I REALLY WANTED TO STAMP OUT WERE INSIDIOUS **INTERNAL** THREATS: PEOPLE WHO **PRETENDED** TO BE ON BOARD WITH THE REVOLUTION WHILE WORKING **SECRETLY** TO DESTROY IT...

FOREIGN SPIES, SECRET FANS OF THE **KING** TRYING TO BRING BACK THE MONARCHY, RICH PEOPLE TRYING TO **HOLD ON** TO THEIR ILL-GOTTEN WEATH...

POOR PEOPLE PUSHING TO GET **TOO MUCH** OF THE RICH PEOPLE'S WEATH, CORRUPT CHEATS LOOKING TO SELL OUT THE REVOLUTION TO MAKE A **QUICK BUCK**...

ONLY WHEN **EVERY LAST ONE** OF THEM HAD BEEN SENT TO THE GUILLOTINE COULD FRANCE FINALLY BECOME A GLORIOUS **REPUBLIC OF VIRTUE.**

AND SO, IN YOUR RELENTLESS QUEST FOR **VIRTUE,** YOU BEGAN THE INFAMOUS **REIGN OF TERROR.**

TERROR IS JUST SWIFT, INFLEXIBLE JUSTICE...

NOT EVEN **DESMOULINS,** YOUR OLD FRIEND, AND INSTIGATOR OF THE STORMING OF THE BASTILLE, WAS SPARED YOUR BRAND OF JUSTICE.

HEY, I **TRIED** TO GET HIM LET OFF! BUT, WELL, HE SHOULDN'T HAVE CRITICISED THE COMMITTEE!

ANY DISUNITY OR DISSENT WAS A THREAT TO THE REVOLUTION.

AT THE HEIGHT OF THE TERROR, THE COMMITTEE WAS CHOPPING OFF OVER **50 HEADS PER DAY.**

WE'RE GONNA NEED A BIGGER BASKET...

BUT THAT WAS KIND OF THE PROBLEM. THERE WERE SO **MANY** PLOTS THAT IT WAS TAKING **FOREVER!** ALL THE TRIALS, EVIDENCE, WITNESSES WE DIDN'T HAVE **TIME** FOR THAT!

SO WE PASSED A LAW DITCHING ALL THAT JUNK. IF A COMMITTEE MEMBER THOUGHT SOMEONE WAS HATCHING A PLOT... BOOM!

GOOD ENOUGH.

BUT WITH THE NEW, NON-EXISTENT STANDARD OF EVIDENCE, PEOPLE COULD JUST **MAKE STUFF UP.**

MAD AT YOUR NEIGHBOUR? JEALOUS OF THAT WOMAN WITH INCREDIBLE HAIR? JUST CLAIM THEY'VE BEEN COMPLAINING ABOUT THE NEW GOVERNMENT AND IT'S OFF TO THE CHOP.

HEH HEH.

CHOP.

CHOP.

CHOP.

WHAT? LOOK, I **TRIED** TO REIN IT IN!

A BIT...

WE HAD THESE ROAMING DELEGATES WHO WENT OUT TO THE PROVINCES TO BRING TERROR TO ANY ENEMIES OF THE REVOLUTION OUT THERE...

AND SOME OF THEM WERE PRETTY BRUTAL. I RECALLED THEM ALL AND STARTED AN **INQUIRY** INTO THE WORST OF THEIR EXCESSES.

WHICH DIDN'T GO DOWN TOO WELL WITH **THEM**. ONE GUY TRIED TO UNDERMINE ME BY SPREADING A RUMOUR I WAS GOING TO MAKE MYSELF A DIVINELY ORDAINED DICTATOR!

AND? WERE YOU?

SHEER NONSENSE. I MEAN... **OKAY**, I HAD THE POWER OF LIFE AND DEATH OVER MILLIONS.

AND, **OKAY**, IN MY CAPACITY AS MORAL GUARDIAN OF THE NATION I HAD JUST INVENTED A NEW **RELIGION**.

YOU WHAT NOW?

THE **CULT OF THE SUPREME BEING**! UNDER **MY** INSPIRED LEADERSHIP, IT WOULD SWEEP OUT THE OLD OPPRESSIVE SUPERSTITIONS, AND USHER IN A NEW LOVE OF VIRTUE, REASON AND THE DIVINE ARCHITECT OF THE UNIVERSE.

OH, AND, **OKAY**, IT'S **ALSO** TRUE I WAS PLANNING A MASSIVE **PURGE** TO GET RID OF ANY OF MY ENEMIES STILL REMAINING IN THE PARLIAMENT.

BUT I THINK I SHOWED **ADMIRABLE** RESTRAINT. I **WARNED** THEM ALL IT WAS COMING, BUT WITHOUT NAMING ANY NAMES.

WELL, THAT "RESTRAINT" MIGHT HAVE BEEN YOUR UNDOING, SINCE EVERY GUY IN THERE FIGURED **HE** COULD BE ON THAT ENEMIES LIST.

ABANDONED BY EVEN THE FEW FRIENDS YOU HAD LEFT, YOU WERE DENOUNCED, ARRESTED AND CONDEMNED.

IN THE END, YOU ENDED YOUR LIFE AS JUST ONE MORE VICTIM OF THE TERRIBLE MACHINE TO WHICH YOU HAD CONDEMNED SO MANY.

I GUESS IN THE END ALL THAT POWER WENT TO YOUR...

WHAT? WENT TO MY WHAT?

THE FRENCH REVOLUTIONARY LEADERS, LIKE **MAXIMILIEN ROBESPIERRE**, WANTED TO IMPROVE **ALL** ASPECTS OF SOCIETY.

LIKE THEY INVENTED NEW RATIONAL WEIGHTS AND MEASURES LIKE THE **METRE** AND THE **KILOGRAM**, WHICH WE **STILL USE**.

AND A NEW, RATIONAL **CALENDAR**, COMPLETE WITH RATIONAL, 10-DAY WEEKS, WHICH WE **DON'T**.

YEEAH... PEOPLE WERE **NOT THRILLED** TO ONLY GET A WEEKEND EVERY **10** DAYS.

SINCE WE'D DITCHED THE OLD CHRISTIAN FESTIVALS, LIKE CHRISTMAS AND EASTER, WE NEEDED SOME NEW ONES. SO I ORGANISED A MASSIVE CEREMONY...

THE FESTIVAL OF THE SUPREME BEING!

THE WHOLE THING BEGAN AT THE **TUILERIES PALACE** (WHERE THE LOUVRE MUSEUM IS NOW), WHERE WE **BURNED** A GIANT STATUE OF ATHEISM TO REVEAL ANOTHER STATUE OF **WISDOM** HIDDEN INSIDE.

THEN ONLOOKERS CHEERED AND THREW CONFETTI AS A MASSIVE PROCESSION OF CITIZENS WOUND ITS WAY THROUGH PARIS TO THE **CHAMPS DE MARS** (WHERE THE EIFFEL TOWER NOW STANDS).

THERE THEY FOUND THE CENTREPIECE OF THE NEW CEREMONY, AN ENORMOUS, PAPIER-MÂCHÉ **MOUNTAIN**.

MY NEXT GUEST IS THE REVOLUTIONARY **FOUNDING FATHER** OF THE **UNITED STATES** OF **AMERICA** (AND THE FACE OF THE DOLLAR BILL).

PLEASE WELCOME THE **QUINTESSENTIAL** ALL-AMERICAN **ACTION HERO** PRESIDENT, IT'S...

GEORGE WASHINGTON!

GEORGE WASHINGTON

U.S. PRESIDENT 1732–1799

WASHINGTON, TO THIS DAY, YOU'RE PROBABLY AMERICA'S BEST KNOWN AND BEST LOVED PRESIDENT. AMERICAN SCHOOLKIDS LEARN BY HEART THE STORIES OF YOUR COURAGE, STRENGTH AND HONESTY, LIKE THE STORY OF THE CHERRY TREE.

WHAT CHERRY TREE?

YOU CUT DOWN YOUR FATHER'S CHERRY TREE, JUST FOR KICKS, I GUESS, BUT WHEN HE CONFRONTED YOU, YOU WERE **SO HONEST** YOU ADMITTED IT...

I CANNOT TELL A LIE...

YEEAH...

NEVER HAPPENED.

AW MAN! REALLY?

I CANNOT TELL A LIE.

WELL, WHAT ABOUT YOUR LEGENDARY FEATS OF STRENGTH!?

LIKE, HOW YOU ONCE THREW A SILVER DOLLAR ACROSS THE POTOMAC RIVER!

THAT'S PRETTY INCREDIBLE.

TOTALLY INCREDIBLE, SINCE THE SILVER DOLLAR HADN'T BEEN INVENTED YET...

BUT THOSE ARE NICE STORIES, EVEN IF THEY'RE NOT TRUE. I ALWAYS WANTED PEOPLE TO SEE ME AS STRONG, COURAGEOUS AND HONEST; THE ESSENTIAL VALUES OF A TRUE **ENGLISH GENTLEMAN.**

BUT... AREN'T YOU **AMERICAN**!?

AMERICA HADN'T BEEN INVENTED YET. WE WERE JOLLY WELL ENGLISH, WHAT, WHAT!

RA-THER.

TOODLE-PIP...

AND I MADE SURE TO LEARN ALL THE ESSENTIAL SKILLS AN ENGLISH GENTLEMAN MUST HAVE: RIDING, FENCING, DANCING!

AND OF COURSE, MY **FAVOURITE** GENTLEMANLY PASTIME: **FIGHTING**! LIKE A TRUE ENGLISHMAN, I SIGNED UP TO FIGHT THE **FRENCH** DURING THE SEVEN YEARS WAR...

LIKE ALL GENTLEMEN OFFICERS, I DRESSED THE PART WITH A TOTALLY SWEET UNIFORM (I DESIGNED IT MYSELF!).

BUT EVEN YOUR AWESOME FASHION SENSE WASN'T ENOUGH TO ATTAIN THE **ULTIMATE** SYMBOL OF GENTLEMANSHIP, A ROYAL COMMISSION IN THE **BRITISH ARMY.**

FRIGHTFULLY SORRY, OLD BEAN. **REAL** ENGLISHMEN ONLY...

HAW HAW!

SO YOU FIGURED IF YOU CAN'T JOIN 'EM, **BEAT 'EM!**

77

WELL, IT TURNS OUT, **LOTS** OF THE COLONISTS THOUGHT THE ENGLISH WERE JERKS.

THOSE ENGLISH ARE **JERKS**!

LIKE, **TOTALLY**.

OMG.

THE ENGLISH HAD STARTED IMPOSING ALL SORTS OF UNFAIR **TAXES**...

IT'S NOT FAIR!

BUT WHAT ARE WE GOING TO **DO** ABOUT IT?!

WHOA! LOOK AT **THAT** GUY!

THAT IS ONE **SWEET** UNIFORM!

WE SHOULD PUT **HIM** IN CHARGE...

HEY! IT WASN'T **JUST** MY AMAZING OUTFITS THAT GOT ME ELECTED COMMANDER-IN-CHIEF OF THE REVOLUTIONARY ARMY! I WAS ALSO A **SUPERB** MILITARY STRATEGIST...

REALLY? COS I HEARD YOU LOST BATTLES **TWICE** AS OFTEN AS YOU WON. THAT'S NOT A GREAT TRACK RECORD...

OH COME ON!

OUR ENEMIES WERE A WELL-FED, WELL-DRESSED, WELL-EQUIPPED, PROFESSIONAL ARMY, FIGHTING FOR THE MOST POWERFUL MAN IN THE WORLD... THE KING OF ENGLAND!

MY GUYS WERE A BEDRAGGLED GROUP OF VOLUNTEERS WITH NO GUNPOWDER, NO SHOES, NO MONEY AND NO MILITARY EXPERIENCE.

BUT I REALISED WE DIDN'T **HAVE** TO WIN ALL THE BATTLES. WE JUST HAD TO **NOT GIVE UP!**

I HELD MY MEN TOGETHER THROUGH DEFEAT AND DREADFUL CONDITIONS BY REMINDING THEM WHAT WE WERE FIGHTING FOR: LIBERTY AND JUSTICE FOR ALL!

AND I USED SNEAKY TACTICS, LIKE CROSSING THE DELAWARE RIVER AT NIGHT, IN A BLIZZARD, TO CATCH OUR ENEMIES UNAWARES.

THEY'LL NEVER SEE US COMING!

MY MEN GREW TOUGHER, AND MORE DISCIPLINED. MORALE INCREASED...

SUPPLIES STARTED ROLLING IN FROM ENGLAND'S GREAT ENEMIES, THE **FRENCH.**

'ERE. 'AVE SOME MUSKETS...

AH 'OPE ZEY KEEL MANY EENGLISH, NON?

AND IN THE END, THE ENGLISH GAVE UP AND WENT HOME!

JOLLY WELL NOT WORTH IT, WHAT?

BALLY YANKEE DOODLES...

YOU WERE THE HERO OF THE NEWLY BORN NATION: THE **UNITED STATES OF AMERICA!**

YOU BECAME **SO** POPULAR, PEOPLE STARTED SUGGESTING **YOU** SHOULD BE KING.

I TOLD THEM NOT TO BE SILLY – WE'D JUST GOTTEN RID OF A KING, WE DIDN'T NEED ANOTHER ONE...

BUT WE NEEDED **SOMEONE** IN CHARGE, OTHERWISE NOTHING WOULD EVER GET DONE.

SO WE INVENTED THE OFFICE OF **PRESIDENT.**

KIND OF A BIT LIKE A KING, BUT **TEMPORARY,** AND **ELECTED BY THE PEOPLE.**

AND THEY WANTED TO ELECT SOMEONE HONOURABLE, SOMEONE TRUSTWORTHY, SOMEONE WELL-DRESSED, SOMEONE TALL...

AND YOU **FIT THE BILL!**

GEDDIT? **BILL?** LIKE DOLLAR BILL...

I GET IT...

DIVISION OF POWERS

AFTER WINNING THE AMERICAN WAR OF INDEPENDENCE, GO-GETTER GENERAL **GEORGE WASHINGTON** FAMOUSLY TRIED TO **RETIRE.**

BUT INSTEAD I GOT HAULED OUT TO OVERSEE THE WRITING OF THE NEW COUNTRY'S FOUNDATIONAL DOCUMENT, THE U.S. **CONSTITUTION.**

A **CONSTITUTION** IS JUST A SET OF LAWS THAT SPELL OUT THE BASIC RULES OF HOW THE GOVERNMENT IS GOING TO WORK.

I ARGUED WE NEEDED A STRONG, CENTRAL GOVERNMENT WITH ENOUGH POWER TO GET STUFF DONE. SORT OF LIKE A KING.

EXCEPT **NOT** A KING SINCE WE'D JUST FINISHED FIGHTING A WAR **SPECIFICALLY** TO GET RID OF THE KING.

SO WE DEVELOPED A SYSTEM OF **CHECKS AND BALANCES,** WHERE EACH **BRANCH** OF THE GOVERNMENT IS IN CHARGE OF DIFFERENT THINGS, AND MAKES SURE THE OTHER PARTS **PLAY NICE.**

THE **LEGISLATIVE BRANCH** IS THE TWO **HOUSES OF CONGRESS.**

THE **SENATE**...

AND THE **HOUSE OF REPRESENTATIVES.**

THEY COME UP WITH **NEW LAWS,** AND IF BOTH HOUSES AGREE ON THEM, THEY TAKE THEM TO THE PRESIDENT FOR SIGNING.

THEY ALSO HAVE THE POWER TO **IMPEACH** THE PRESIDENT AND KICK HIM OUT OF OFFICE IF HE GETS OUT OF LINE.

CONGRESS CAN ALSO PUT FORWARD **AMENDMENTS** TO THE CONSTITUTION – REVISIONS THAT ADD NEW BITS OR CHANGE WHAT'S IN THERE ALREADY.

FOR EXAMPLE, THE **13TH AMENDMENT** FINALLY ABOLISHED SLAVERY IN **1865.**

OH GOOD, I HOPED THEY'D DO AWAY WITH THAT – NASTY BUSINESS.

YOU OWNED **317** SLAVES!

I SET THEM ALL FREE!

AFTER I WAS DEAD, SURE, BUT STILL....

THE **EXECUTIVE BRANCH** IS BASICALLY THE **PRESIDENT**.

THE PRESIDENT IS A SORT OF KING-SUBSTITUTE, BUT **ELECTED**, AND ONLY FOR **4** YEARS, AFTER WHICH THERE'S ANOTHER ELECTION.

THE PRESIDENT IS IN CHARGE OF MAKING **PEACE OR WAR** WITH OTHER COUNTRIES.

I NOBLY AND DUTIFULLY AGREED TO BE ELECTED THE FIRST ONE...

AND HIS **SIGNATURE** IS REQUIRED TO MAKE LAWS OFFICIAL (WHICH MEANS HE CAN ALSO **VETO** (BLOCK) LAWS HE DOESN'T LIKE.

I BELIEVED THE PRESIDENT ALSO HAS A RESPONSIBILITY AS A SORT OF NATIONAL **ROLE-MODEL**, SO I TRIED TO DEMONSTRATE THE SORT OF DIGNIFIED, HONOURABLE BEHAVIOUR I WANTED TO SEE IN OTHERS.

THE **JUDICIAL BRANCH** IS THE LAW COURTS.

THEY ARE THE **JUDGES** WHO INTERPRET WHAT THE LAW MEANS IN ACTUAL TRIALS.

AT THE VERY TOP IS THE **SUPREME COURT**, WHICH JUDGES THOSE CASES TOO DIFFICULT OR IMPORTANT FOR THE OTHERS TO HANDLE.

THEY ARE APPOINTED BY THE PRESIDENT, BUT HAVE TO BE APPROVED BY THE SENATE.

THEY CAN ALSO **BLOCK** THE PRESIDENT OR CONGRESS FROM DOING SOMETHING **UNCONSTITUTIONAL** (BREAKING THE RULES IN THE CONSTITUTION).

LOTS OF COUNTRIES IN THE WORLD HAVE A CONSTITUTION...

I GUESS IT WAS WORTH GETTING OUT OF YOUR DRESSING GOWN AFTER ALL...

BUT THE U.S. CONSTITUTION WAS THE **FIRST** COMPLETELY WRITTEN NATIONAL CONSTITUTION, AND IT REMAINS THE OLDEST ONE **STILL IN USE**, ANYWHERE IN THE WORLD.

AND NOW LET'S MEET THE **BUTT-KICKING BOOKWORM** WHO **FOUGHT** THE FRENCH, **SMASHED** THE SPANISH AND **BASHED** THE BRITISH TO FOUND THE WORLD'S FIRST (AND ONLY) **FREE REPUBLIC** OF FORMER SLAVES.

HE'S THE **HEROIC HEAD HONCHO** OF THE HAITIAN REVOLUTION, IT'S...

TOUSSAINT LOUVERTURE!

TOUSSAINT LOUVERTURE
REBEL LEADER
1743–1803

TOUSSAINT, YOU WERE BORN INTO PERHAPS THE MOST CRUEL, BRUTAL AND INHUMAN OF ALL THE NEW WORLD SLAVE COLONIES, FRENCH OCCUPIED SAINT-DOMINGUE. (LATER RESTORED TO ITS ORIGINAL NAME: 'HAITI'.)

MORE THAN A MILLION AFRICANS WERE STOLEN FROM THEIR HOMES TO BE BEATEN, STARVED AND WORKED TO DEATH ON HAITI'S HUGE SUGAR PLANTATIONS.

MOST DIED WITHIN **2** YEARS OF THEIR ARRIVAL, SINCE IT WAS CHEAPER TO JUST **IMPORT** NEW SLAVES THAN TO KEEP OLD ONES ALIVE.

I WAS ACTUALLY PRETTY LUCKY, IF YOU CAN EVER CALL A SLAVE "LUCKY". MY FATHER HAD BEEN A PRINCE BEFORE HE WAS CAPTURED AND SOLD BY HIS ENEMIES.

SO, WHILE I WAS STILL A **SLAVE**, I LEARNED TO READ AND WRITE, AND WAS GIVEN SOME OF THE BETTER JOBS. YOU KNOW, THE KIND THAT DIDN'T INVOLVE BEING **WHIPPED** ALL THE TIME...

PLUS I HAD ACCESS TO MY MASTER'S EXPENSIVE **LIBRARY**, WHICH ALLOWED ME TO CONTINUE MY EDUCATION WITH SOME OF HISTORY'S **GREATEST** TEACHERS...

GUYS LIKE **JULIUS CAESAR** (MILITARY TACTICS), **MACHIAVELLI** (POLITICAL THEORY) AND **EPICTETUS** (THE GREEK STOIC PHILOSOPHER WHO HAD HIMSELF BEEN A SLAVE).

AND I ALSO DISCOVERED THE MORE RECENT THINKERS OF THE FRENCH ENLIGHTENMENT. GUYS LIKE **ROUSSEAU**, WHO ARGUED THAT ALL MEN ARE CREATED EQUAL.

WHICH BASICALLY PROVES THAT SLAVERY IS RUBBISH.

HMM. I WAS JUST THINKING THAT...

THAT MIGHT SEEM PRETTY OBVIOUS TO YOU NOW, BUT AT THE TIME IS WAS CONSIDERED A **DANGEROUS** IDEA.

DANGEROUS? HOW COULD **EQUALITY** BE DANGEROUS?

WELL, IT GOT THE FRENCH TO OVERTHROW THEIR ARISTOCRACY AND KILL THEIR KING. SO I GUESS IT WAS PRETTY DANGEROUS FOR **THEM**...

THE FRENCH REVOLUTION ALSO THREW HAITI INTO CHAOS, WITH PRO-REVOLUTION FOLKS FIGHTING SUPPORTERS OF THE MONARCHY.

VIVE LA FRANCE!

VIVE LE ROI!

AND THEN, TAKING ADVANTAGE OF THE CONFUSION, AN ESCAPED VOUDOU PRIEST NAMED **DUTTY BOUKMAN** COORDINATED A MASSIVE SLAVE REVOLT.

AT THE SAME EXACT MOMENT, SLAVES ACROSS HAITI ROSE UP, SET FIRE TO THE PLANTATIONS, GRABBED WHATEVER FARM TOOLS THEY COULD, AND TOOK THEIR VIOLENT REVENGE ON EVERY WHITE PERSON THEY COULD FIND.

FOR THREE WEEKS, THE SMOKE FROM BURNING PLANTATIONS BLOTTED OUT THE SUN.

BUT WHILE RAGE AND HATE MADE THEM STRONG, IT ALSO MADE THEM WEAK. THEY WERE DISORGANISED, WITH NO PLAN, NO WEAPONS AND NO SUPPLIES.

THE SLAVE OWNERS STOPPED FIGHTING EACH OTHER AND GANGED UP TO SUPPRESS THE REBELLION. BOUKMAN, THE REBEL LEADER, WAS CAPTURED AND HIS HEAD PUT ON A SPIKE.

THINGS WERE LOOKING BAD FOR THE REBELLION. THEY NEEDED A **LEADER**, SOMEONE WHO UNDERSTOOD THE TACTICS, POLITICS AND PHILOSOPHY OF THE EUROPEANS.

UH. HELLO...?

I KNOW, RIGHT?

I STARTED SMALL, RECRUITING JUST A FEW HUNDRED MEN AND TRAINING THEM IN MILITARY TACTICS AND DISCIPLINE.

INSTEAD OF AN ANGRY MOB, THEY WERE BECOMING AN **ARMY**. THE DISCIPLINE TO WAIT FOR ORDERS BEFORE ATTACKING MEANT WE COULD SET AMBUSHES...

AND THE DISCIPLINE **NOT** TO KILL MEANT OUR ENEMIES WOULD SURRENDER INSTEAD OF FIGHTING TO THE DEATH.

AND I ALSO USED MY UNDERSTANDING OF POLITICS TO MAKE AN ALLIANCE WITH THE NEIGHBOURING **SPANISH** (WHO HATED THE FRENCH) TO GET MY HANDS ON FRESH WEAPONS AND SUPPLIES.

YOU WON BATTLE AFTER BATTLE, DEFEATING THE FRENCH **AND** YOUR ENEMIES AMONG THE REBELS, TO BECOME LEADER OF THE WHOLE EX-SLAVE ARMY.

BUT THEN, JUST WHEN YOU HAD THE FRENCH ALMOST COMPLETELY BEATEN, YOU SUDDENLY SWITCHED SIDES AND STARTED FIGHTING **FOR** THEM!

WHAT THE HELL, MAN?

WELL, IT WASN'T QUITE THE SAME FRENCH; A NEW, RADICAL GROUP HAD TAKEN OVER, AND **THEY** PROMISED TO ABOLISH SLAVERY COMPLETELY.

WHEREAS THE **SPANISH** REALLY JUST WANTED US TO BEAT THE FRENCH, SO **THEY** COULD COME IN, TAKE OVER AND MAKE US ALL SLAVES AGAIN.

SO YOU FOUGHT OFF THE SPANISH...

AND THE BRITISH, WHO JUST SHOWED UP HOPING TO GRAB SOME LAND FOR THEMSELVES IN THE CONFUSION.

BUT THE OUTSIDE WORLD WAS EVEN **MORE** CONFUSING. IN THE CHAOS FOLLOWING THE FRENCH REVOLUTION, A RUTHLESS GENERAL NAMED **NAPOLEON** HAD TAKEN CONTROL.

HE WANTED TO RECONQUER THE ISLAND AND REINSTATE SLAVERY. NO **WAY** I WAS GOING TO LET THAT HAPPEN!

NAPOLEON'S ARMY WAS TOO BIG TO FIGHT HEAD-ON, SO ONCE AGAIN I GOT **TACTICAL**, HIDING IN THE MOUNTAINS AND ALLOWING HORRIBLE TROPICAL DISEASES LIKE **YELLOW FEVER** TO TAKE THEM OUT **FOR** ME...

OOH. CUNNING...

BUT I WAS GETTING TIRED. I'D BEEN FIGHTING FOR **10** YEARS, BUT ALL I REALLY WANTED TO DO WAS TO RETIRE, HANG OUT WITH MY FAMILY AND POTTER IN MY GARDEN.

THE FRENCH OFFERED TO NEGOTIATE PEACE, BUT THEN HAD ME CAPTURED AND SHIPPED OFF TO DIE IN PRISON.

BUT I KNEW, EVEN IF THEY KILLED ME, THEY'D ONLY BE CUTTING DOWN THE **TRUNK** OF THE TREE OF FREEDOM! ITS ROOTS WERE TOO DEEP TO **EVER** BE DESTROYED...

THE HAITIAN PEOPLE CONTINUED THE FIGHT AND, WITHIN **MONTHS** OF YOUR DEATH, WON THEIR FREEDOM.

I GUESS YOU COULD SAY THEY JUST... **WOODEN** QUIT...?

TREE...? WOODEN...?

-SIGH-

I SPOKE WITH **TOUISSAINT LOUVERTURE** ABOUT HIS STRUGGLE TO FREE THE SLAVES OF WHAT IS NOW **HAITI**. BUT WHAT WERE ALL THOSE SLAVES EVEN **DOING THERE** IN THE FIRST PLACE!?

RIGHT, WELL IN HAITI IT WAS MOSTLY ABOUT **SUGAR**. SOME MERCHANTS REALISED THEY COULD MAKE A **FORTUNE** SELLING THE STUFF TO THE SWEET-TOOTHED EUROPEANS, AND SO THEY DEVELOPED SOMETHING CALLED THE **TRIANGULAR TRADE**.

MOST SLAVES ENDURED BACK-BREAKING LABOUR, CLEARING, PLANTING, TENDING AND HARVESTING THE SUGAR CANE FIELDS OF THE PLANTATIONS. MOST DIED WITHIN **10** YEARS FROM OVERWORK, DISEASE, AND CRUEL PUNISHMENTS FOR THE SMALLEST INFRACTIONS.

IN THE FINAL SIDE OF THE TRIANGLE, THE **"RETURN PASSAGE"**, PLANTATION-PRODUCED SUGAR, COTTON AND TOBACCO WERE SHIPPED BACK TO EUROPE TO BE PROCESSED AND SOLD, AND THE WHOLE CYCLE BEGAN AGAIN.

HALF A MILLION WENT TO NORTH AMERICA.

2 MILLION WENT TO BRITISH COLONIES LIKE JAMAICA.

STOP 3: THE NEW WORLD

OVER **10 MILLION** AFRICANS WERE SHIPPED TO THE NEW WORLD AS SLAVES.

1.5 MILLION WERE SHIPPED TO FRENCH SAINT-DOMINGUE (HAITI), INCLUDING MY PARENTS.

2.5 MILLION WENT TO THE MASSIVE SPANISH EMPIRE.

4 MILLION WENT TO THE PORTUGUESE EMPIRE, IN WHAT IS NOW BRAZIL.

THE MAGNIFICENT MAROONS

DESPITE THE HORRIBLE PUNISHMENTS IF THEY WERE CAUGHT, SOME SLAVES DID MANAGE TO ESCAPE INTO THE UNINHABITED MOUNTAINS OF JAMAICA AND HAITI, AND THE JUNGLES OF BRAZIL.

THE LARGEST OF THESE COMMUNITIES OF "MAROONS" (ESCAPED SLAVES) WAS THE **QUILOMBO DOS PALMARES** IN BRAZIL. AT ITS HEIGHT IT CONTAINED OVER **20,000** PEOPLE WITH THEIR OWN KING.

BUT **MY** REBELLION WAS THE **ONLY ONE** THAT LED TO A PERMANENT, FREE COUNTRY OF FORMER SLAVES.

TRIANGLE of TEARS
STOP 1: EUROPE

ON THE FIRST LEG OF THE JOURNEY, TRADING SHIPS SET OUT CARRYING THE SORT OF MANUFACTURED GOODS EUROPE SPECIALISED IN; THINGS LIKE CLOTH, CUTLERY, RUM AND ESPECIALLY GUNS. **LOTS** OF GUNS.

THE TRIANGULAR TRADE CONSISTED OF THREE MAIN SEA VOYAGES TO THREE DIFFERENT LOCATIONS.

THE PORTUGUESE BEGAN THE TRANS-ATLANTIC SLAVE TRADE, BUT IT DIDN'T TAKE LONG FOR OTHER COUNTRIES TO GET IN ON THE ACT. PARTICULARLY **BRITAIN**, WHO BECAME THE INDUSTRY LEADER, ENSLAVING MORE AFRICANS THAN ANYWHERE ELSE.

STOP 2: AFRICA

THE SHIPS TRADED THEIR GUNS TO AFRICAN COASTAL NATIONS LIKE THE **ASANTE**, **OYO** AND **DAHOMENY**, WHO USED THEM TO DEFEAT THEIR ENEMIES AND TAKE THEM PRISONER.

THE VICTORS MARCHED THEIR CAPTIVES TO **SLAVE FORTS** ALONG THE COAST; CASTLES WHERE SLAVES WERE KEPT CHAINED UP UNTIL A SHIP CAME ALONG TO BUY THEM.

THEN BEGAN THE MOST HORRENDOUS PORTION OF THE WHOLE HORRIBLE BUSINESS, A TWO-MONTH-LONG OCEAN JOURNEY KNOWN AS "**THE MIDDLE PASSAGE**".

THE SLAVE TRADE, AND THE DAMAGE IT DID TO AFRICAN PEOPLE, REMAINS ONE OF THE MOST MASSIVE AND HORRIFIC ATROCITIES IN HUMAN HISTORY.

MEDICINE MAN, WAR CHIEF, VISIONARY, AS WELL AS THE LAST CHIEF OF THE GREAT **SIOUX NATION** TO LAY DOWN HIS RIFLE AND MAKE PEACE WITH THE UNITED STATES OF AMERICA...

PLEASE WELCOME **TATANKA IYOTAKE,** BETTER KNOWN AS...

SITTING BULL!

SITTING BULL
SIOUX LEADER
1831-1890

SITTING BULL, YOUR CRUSHING DEFEAT OF U.S. ARMY GENERAL GEORGE CUSTER AT THE BATTLE OF THE LITTLE BIGHORN WAS THE GREATEST SIOUX VICTORY IN THE WHOLE HISTORY OF THE WILD WEST.

WHICH IS ALL THE MORE SURPRISING SINCE YOU WERE REALLY FAMOUS NOT AS A WAR CHIEF, BUT AS A MEDICINE MAN. IS THAT LIKE A DOCTOR?

HMM, NOT REALLY. A MEDICINE MAN OR WOMAN MIGHT DO SOME HEALING, BUT THE WORD YOU WHITES TRANSLATED AS "MEDICINE" REALLY MEANS SOMETHING MORE LIKE "SACRED MYSTERY".

SO A **MEDICINE MAN** IS ONE WHO TRIES TO SPEAK WITH, AND TO UNDERSTAND, THE GREAT SACRED MYSTERY THAT CREATES AND PERMEATES THE WORLD.

SOUNDS... MYSTERIOUS...

YEAH, WELL, A LOT OF HOW WE THOUGHT DIDN'T MAKE MUCH SENSE TO YOU WHITE MEN.

AND VICE VERSA.

FOR EXAMPLE, AS SETTLERS MOVED INTO OUR COUNTRY, THEY STARTED FENCING OFF THE LAND WHERE OUR ANCESTORS HAD ONCE ROAMED FREELY.

THIS IS **MINE** NOW, INJUN!

HOW CAN YOU SAY YOU **OWN** LAND — THE GIFT OF THE GREAT MYSTERY!? MIGHT AS WELL SAY YOU **OWN** THE SKY! HERE — THIS IS **MY** BIT OF SKY! DON'T LOOK AT IT!

RIDICULOUS. BUT TO MAKE MATTERS WORSE, THE MASSIVE BUFFALO HERDS OF THE PLAINS WERE AN **INCONVENIENCE** TO THE SETTLERS AND THE NEWLY BUILT RAILROADS.

THEY ORGANISED TRAIN-MOUNTED SHOOTING PARTIES TO KILL THE BUFFALO OFF. DIDN'T EVEN EAT THEM, JUST LEFT 'EM TO ROT!

WOO! YEE-HAW!

BANG! BANG!

THAT'S **INSANE**. THE GREAT MYSTERY CREATED THE WORLD FOR HUMANS AND ANIMALS TO LIVE IN **TOGETHER**! SURE, WE HUNTED BUFFALO, BUT ONLY FOR OUR **DINNER**.

WHICH IS ANOTHER GOOD POINT. WITHOUT THE BUFFALO WE HAD NOTHING TO **EAT**.

THE U.S. GOVERNMENT PROPOSED **RESERVING** SOME LAND ESPECIALLY FOR US, SO NO SETTLERS WOULD BE ALLOWED AND THEY'D PROVIDE US WITH FOOD TO MAKE UP FOR THE LOST BUFFALO.

THAT SOUNDS... NICE...?

OH **SURE**, WHY ROAM THE VAST **FREEDOM** OF THE GREAT PLAINS WHEN WE COULD LIVE **IMPRISONED** BEHIND FENCES AT THE MERCY OF WHITE MEN WHO **NEVER KEEP THEIR PROMISES**!

LIKE THE BLACK HILLS?

LIKE THE BLACK HILLS. OUR MOST HOLY PLACE. I MEAN, IT'S ONLY THE **SACRED CENTRE** OF THE **WHOLE WORLD**!

THE GOVERNMENT PROMISED THAT, IF WE STAYED ON THE RESERVATIONS, THEY'D LEAVE THE BLACK HILLS ALONE. WHICH I DIDN'T BELIEVE FOR A **SECOND**.

TURNS OUT, THERE WAS **GOLD** IN THEM THAR HILLS. BEFORE YOU KNEW IT, THE WHOLE PLACE WAS **CRAWLING** WITH ILLEGAL, GREEDY GOLD-PROSPECTORS!

AND, INSTEAD OF KICKING THEM OUT, THE GOVERNMENT SENT AN ARMY TO PROTECT THEM AND **ARREST** US!

THESE **SAVAGES** DON'T STAND A CHANCE AGAINST A **MODERN** ARMY!

GENERAL CUSTER

SOUNDS LIKE TROUBLE. WHAT DID YOU DO?

I CALLED A GATHERING OF THE TRIBES BESIDE THE **LITTLE BIGHORN RIVER**, AND PRAYED TO THE GREAT MYSTERY FOR GUIDANCE.

I CUT MY ARMS **100** TIMES AND DANCED, WITHOUT FOOD OR WATER, FOR DAYS, STARING INTO THE SUN, UNTIL I COLLAPSED.

WHOA. THAT'S QUITE A SERIOUS PRAYER...

YEAH, WELL, I **SERIOUSLY** NEEDED TO TALK TO THE GREAT MYSTERY.

IN MY TRANCE, I SAW A **VISION**. A TROOP OF SOLDIERS ON HORSEBACK, FALLING UPSIDE-DOWN INTO A VILLAGE OF TIPIS.

I TOOK IT TO BE A PREDICTION OF THE FUTURE. OUR BRAVES COULD GO INTO BATTLE **CERTAIN** THE ENEMY WOULD FALL, AS THE VISION FORETOLD.

AND WHEN CUSTER'S FORCES, CARELESS AND OVER-CONFIDENT, TRIED TO CHARGE YOUR ENCAMPMENT, THAT'S EXACTLY WHAT HAPPENED!

THE BATTLE OF THE LITTLE BIGHORN **UTTERLY OBLITERATED** A U.S. ARMY THAT THOUGHT ITSELF **UNBEATABLE**! HOW'D IT FEEL?

UM... NOT GREAT, ACTUALLY. THEY JUST SENT ANOTHER, BIGGER ARMY. I BEGAN TO REALISE WE MIGHT'VE WON THE BATTLE, BUT WE COULDN'T WIN THE WAR.

STARVING TO DEATH, AND WITH NOWHERE TO GO, I DIDN'T NEED A **VISION** TO PREDICT THE ONLY WAY TO SAVE MY PEOPLE WAS TO SURRENDER...

WITH YOUR ARREST AND TRANSFER ONTO THE RESERVATIONS, AMERICA COULD FINALLY CONSIDER THE WEST TO BE **WON**.

BUT YOUR ADVENTURES WEREN'T QUITE OVER YET. BORED WITH LIVING OFF HANDOUTS ON THE RESERVATION, YOU BEGAN A BIZARRE SECOND CAREER AS A TOURIST ATTRACTION.

YEAH, I AGREED TO JOIN BUFFALO BILL'S **WILD WEST SHOW**, A SORT OF TRAVELLING CIRCUS FEATURING FAMOUS PEOPLE FROM WHAT WAS NOW THE **OLD** WEST.

ALL I HAD TO DO WAS WEAR MY WAR-BONNET AND RIDE AROUND A FEW TIMES (AND PUT UP WITH BEING BOOED AND HISSED AT).

I WAS SHOCKED BY WHAT THEY CALLED "CIVILISATION". THE WHITE MAN'S VILLAGES HAD **SO MANY** PEOPLE IT MADE MY HEAD SPIN.

AND THEY HAD SO MUCH **STUFF**. BUT EVERYWHERE I WENT I SAW **MASSES** OF PEOPLE LIVING IN JUST **ABJECT** POVERTY.

THEY CALLED **US** SAVAGES, BUT **NO** SIOUX WOULD LEAVE PEOPLE TO **STARVE** WHEN HE HAD FOOD TO GIVE THEM.

I ALWAYS SAID: "THE WHITE MAN KNOWS HOW TO MAKE EVERYTHING, BUT HE DOES NOT KNOW HOW TO DISTRIBUTE IT."

-AHEM-

SPEAKING OF WHICH...

COUNTING COUP

WE'VE JUST MET **SITTING BULL**, THE LAKOTA SIOUX CHIEF WHOSE **VISIONARY** LEADERSHIP INSPIRED THE LEGENDARY **BATTLE OF THE LITTLE BIGHORN.**

BUT I DIDN'T GET THE CHANCE TO ASK HIM ABOUT ONE OF THE MOST DISTINCTIVE AND RECOGNISABLE TRADITIONS OF PLAINS TRIBES LIKE THE SIOUX, THE **EAGLE-FEATHER WAR-BONNET.**

THE COUP IS WHERE YOU JUST **TOUCH** AN ENEMY WITH YOUR HAND OR **COUP STICK** IN THE MIDDLE OF A BATTLE. SORT OF LIKE A GAME OF **TAG**, ONLY MORE DANGEROUS.

WHEN A YOUNG BRAVE COUNTS HIS FIRST COUP HE BECOMES A WARRIOR, AND IS PERMITTED TO WEAR A SINGLE EAGLE FEATHER TO COMMEMORATE THE ACHIEVEMENT.

DIFFERENT TYPES OF FEATHERS INDICATE DIFFERENT ACHIEVEMENTS

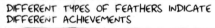

| ENEMY KILLED | WEARER INJURED | WEARER INJURED A LOT | TOOK ENEMY SCALP | CUT ENEMY THROAT |

IN MY DAY, THE SIOUX WERE A WARRIOR SOCIETY. YOUNG MEN ACHIEVED SUCCESS AND RENOWN BY FIGHTING OTHER TRIBES, LIKE OUR OLD ENEMIES, THE CROW AND PAWNEE.

BUT KILLING A MAN IS ACTUALLY PRETTY EASY: YOU CAN JUST SHOOT HIM. WHERE'S THE HONOUR IN THAT?

BY FAR THE **MOST** PRESTIGIOUS ACHIEVEMENT WAS THE **COUP** (PRONOUNCED "COO" – FROM THE FRENCH WORD FOR A BLOW OR STRIKE).

SOME OLD WARRIORS COUNTED SO MANY COUPS IN THEIR LIVES THEY NEEDED SOME SORT OF HEAD-GEAR TO WEAR THEM ALL. AND SO THE WAR-BONNET WAS BORN.

FEATHERS WERE SUPER IMPORTANT IN SIOUX SOCIETY BECAUSE THEY ALLOWED THE WEARER TO TELL EVERYONE THE STORY OF HOW HE EARNED THEM. SO THEY WOULD KNOW HOW TOTALLY AWESOME HE WAS.

YOU COULD ALSO COUNT A COUP FOR OTHER ACTS OF DARING, LIKE STEALING A HORSE, DISARMING AN ENEMY, OR SAVING A FELLOW WARRIOR.

I COUNTED MY OWN FIRST COUP ON A RAID AGAINST THE CROW WHEN I WAS JUST **14**.

BY THE TIME I WAS AN OLD MAN, I HAD OVER **60** COUPS TO MY NAME.

TALK ABOUT FEATHERS IN YOUR CAP!

MY NEXT GUEST IS ONE OF HISTORY'S MOST DE-**VOTE**-ED CAMPAIGNERS FOR **WOMEN'S RIGHTS!**

IT'S THE **SPECTACULAR SUFFRAGETTE** LEADER...

EMMELINE PANKHURST!

EMMELINE PANKHURST

SUFFRAGETTE LEADER

1858—1928

MRS PANKHURST, YOU DEDICATED YOUR LIFE TO WINNING THE RIGHT TO VOTE FOR WOMEN, WHY WAS **THAT** SO IMPORTANT?

WHY WAS IT SO... **YOUNG MAN!** IT'S THE **MOST IMPORTANT** THING!

IN A **DEMOCRACY**, LIKE BRITAIN IS SUPPOSED TO BE, PEOPLE HAVE **ONE WAY** TO HAVE A SAY IN HOW THINGS ARE RUN, AND THAT IS TO **VOTE.**

IF YOU DON'T HAVE A VOTE, NO ONE NEED TO LISTEN TO **ANYTHING** YOU SAY. THAT MEANS YOU ARE NOT A **PERSON**, YOU ARE **PROPERTY**.

WOMEN HAD BEEN TRYING FOR **YEARS** TO GET THE VOTE, BUT SINCE THEY DIDN'T **HAVE** THE VOTE, THE GOVERNMENT DIDN'T NEED TO LISTEN TO THEM.

"Dear Prime Minister, women think that..."

HA HA HA HA!

SO, ALONG WITH MY DAUGHTERS, I FOUNDED A NEW, RADICAL ORGANISATION DETERMINED TO DO **WHATEVER IT TOOK** TO WIN WOMEN'S **SUFFRAGE** (THE RIGHT TO VOTE).

WE NAMED OURSELVES THE **WOMEN'S SOCIAL AND POLITICAL UNION**, BUT BEFORE LONG EVERYONE JUST CALLED US **SUFFRAGETTES**.

IT WAS SUPPOSED TO BE A DEMEANING NICKNAME, BUT WE QUICKLY REALISED IT WAS **WAY CATCHIER**.

I MEAN, COME ON! WOMEN'S SOCIAL AND POLITICAL UNION? WHAT A MOUTHFUL!

I TOOK TO THE ROAD TO WHIP UP SUPPORT FOR OUR NEW PLAN OF DIRECT-ACTION PROTEST TACTICS.

SISTERS! THE GOVERNMENT REFUSES TO LISTEN! THE TIME FOR WORDS IS OVER! NOW IS THE TIME FOR **DEEDS**!

HEAR HEAR!

HURRAH!

WE STARTED BY BREAKING WINDOWS, LIKE THE PRIME MINISTER'S AT **10** DOWNING STREET.

EGAD!

I USED TO SAY THAT "THE BROKEN WINDOW IS THE MOST PERSUASIVE ARGUMENT IN MODERN POLITICS".

WE CHAINED OURSELVES TO THE RAILINGS OUTSIDE PARLIAMENT.

HOW EMBARRASSING!

FOR **THEM**! THEY COULDN'T IGNORE US, THEN!

FROM THERE, WE HIT THEM WHERE IT **REALLY** HURTS. IN THE **GOLF COURSE!**

BURNED WITH ACID

VOTES FOR WOMEN

OH, AND PUNCHING POLICEMEN. I ALWAYS LIKED THAT...

BIFF!

NOT **HARD**, YOU KNOW... JUST SO WE'D GET ARRESTED.

YOU **WANTED** TO GET ARRESTED?

WE WANTED TO SHOW THAT WE WERE NOT PREPARED TO BE GOVERNED BY LAWS ON WHICH WE WERE NOT CONSULTED.

SO THEY PUT US IN JAIL. I MYSELF WAS ARRESTED SEVEN OR EIGHT TIMES.

THEY THOUGHT THAT WOULD SHUT US UP! BUT WE CONTINUED TO FIGHT IN THE ONLY WAY LEFT TO US — **HUNGER STRIKE!**

IT WOULD HAVE LOOKED BAD IF SUFFRAGETTES STARTED **DYING** IN PRISON, SO THE GOVERNMENT RELEASED US...

HUNGRY, MRS PANKHURST?

OH, I COULD EAT A HORSE.

...ONLY TO ARREST US AGAIN AS SOON AS WE HAD RECOVERED.

FEELING BETTER, MRS PANKHURST?

-COFF- STILL VERY WEAK, OFFICER...

ALL OF WHICH MADE IT MOST INCONVENIENT FOR ME TO GIVE SPEECHES, SINCE NOW THE POLICE WERE WAITING WHEREVER I WENT.

OK, **NOW** YOU'RE BETTER...

I HAD TO RELY ON MY JIU-JITSU-TRAINED SUFFRAGETTE BODYGUARDS TO KEEP THEM AT BAY.

HOLD ON, DID YOU JUST SAY **JIU-JITSU-TRAINED SUFFRAGETTE BODYGUARDS!?**

WELL, AS OUR NOTORIETY GREW, THE POLICE, AND EVEN ANGRY MEMBERS OF THE PUBLIC, BEGAN TO GET REALLY QUITE VIOLENT.

GET BACK IN THE KITCHEN!

SO I ENCOURAGED ALL SUFFRAGETTES TO LEARN SELF-DEFENCE, EVEN RECRUITING ONE OF BRITAIN'S FIRST WOMEN MARTIAL ARTISTS, **EDITH GARRUD**, TO TRAIN THEM.

JIU-JITSU, A JAPANESE UNARMED COMBAT SYSTEM, WAS IDEAL FOR WOMEN, SINCE IT SPECIALISES IN USING AN OPPONENT'S STRENGTH AGAINST THEM.

WE DIDN'T START THIS FIGHT. BUT WE WERE READY TO DO **ANYTHING** TO END IT.

ALMOST ANYTHING.

WELL YES, IN **1914** THE FIRST WORLD WAR BROKE OUT, AND THAT CHANGED THINGS...

THE THREAT WAS **SO GREAT**, THAT I CALLED FOR A TOTAL SUSPENSION OF SUFFRAGETTE ACTIVITY, SO EVERYONE COULD PULL TOGETHER TO WIN THE WAR.

WITH ALL THE MEN AWAY FIGHTING, WOMEN HAD TO DO THEIR JOBS.

SO IN THE END IT WAS A **COMBINATION** OF THE SUFFRAGETTES, THE WAR AND JUST THE CHANGING TIMES...

BUT EITHER WAY, WOMEN DID FINALLY GET THE RIGHT TO VOTE.

AND I'M SURE ALL THE WOMEN OF BRITAIN WOULD OFFER YOU A **VOTE** OF **THANKS!**

NO JOB FOR A LADY?

SOCIETY-SHAPING SUFFRAGETTE **EMMELINE PANKHURST** SAW THE ROLE OF WOMEN RADICALLY REVISED BY THE ONSET OF **WORLD WAR 1**.

THE WAR CHANGED **EVERYTHING**.

HOW COULD IT **NOT**, WHEN SO MANY MEN WERE AWAY, AND SO MANY NEVER CAME BACK?

WITH MILLIONS OF JOBS **LEFT EMPTY** BY THE MEN WHO'D GONE TO FIGHT, THERE WAS REALLY NO **OPTION** BUT TO LET WOMEN DO THEM.

ALMOST A **MILLION** WOMEN WENT INTO **MUNITIONS FACTORIES**, PRODUCING VAST QUANTITIES OF GUNS, PLANES, BOMBS AND BULLETS.

MUNITIONETTES WERE RELATIVELY WELL PAID, BUT THE WORK WAS UNPLEASANT AND DANGEROUS.

TNT EXPLOSIVES ARE **LETHALLY TOXIC**, NOT TO MENTION ALL THE **POISON GAS** THE ARMY USED BACK THEN.

AND OF COURSE, EXPLOSIVES **EXPLODE**. SEVERAL MUNITIONS FACTORIES WENT UP IN SMOKE, TAKING THEIR MUNITIONETTES WITH THEM.

A QUARTER OF A MILLION WOMEN VOLUNTEERED FOR THE **WOMEN'S LAND ARMY**, AND WERE HIRED OUT AS CHEAP LABOUR TO FARMERS.

FARMERETTES (YES, THEY REALLY LIKED THE -ETTE SUFFIX BACK THEN) BASICALLY **REPLACED** FARM MACHINERY, LIKE TRACTORS, SO THE ARMY COULD USE THE **FUEL**.

THE FIRST WOMEN **POLICE OFFICERS** WERE EMPLOYED DURING **WW1**, AS WERE THE FIRST FIREFIGHTERS, BUS DRIVERS, TICKET COLLECTORS AND POSTAL WORKERS.

GO ON, PAL. CALL ME "OFFICERETTE" - I DARE YA...

OVER **100,000** JOINED THE **WOMEN'S ARMY AUXILIARY CORPS**, AND ITS SISTER BRANCHES IN THE NAVY AND AIR FORCE. THEY TOOK OVER NON-COMBAT ARMY JOBS LIKE COOKING, DRIVING, MECHANIC DUTIES AND OFFICE WORK, FREEING UP MORE MEN TO FIGHT.

DURING THE WAR, IT WAS ALL ABOUT WOMEN DOING **WHATEVER IT TOOK** FOR GOD AND COUNTRY.

BUT IT WAS A DIFFERENT STORY WHEN THE WAR ENDED...

THE MEN COMING HOME WERE AFRAID THEY'D BEEN REPLACED.

BUT THEY NEEDN'T HAVE WORRIED. IN MOST CASES, WOMEN WERE UNCEREMONIOUSLY KICKED OUT AND TOLD TO GO BACK TO THE KITCHEN.

BUT THEIR SACIFICE, DEDICATION AND OBVIOUS COMPETENCE IN THE WORKFORCE DIDN'T GO **ENTIRELY** UNREWARDED...

THE GOVERNMENT FINALLY GAVE WOMEN THE RIGHT TO VOTE IN **1918**, JUST AFTER THE WAR ENDED.

WELL... RICH WOMEN OVER **30** GOT IT IN **1918**. EVERYONE ELSE HAD TO WAIT ANOTHER **10** YEARS. BUT THEY GOT IT EVENTUALLY...

MY NEXT GUEST IS THE MAN WHO TOOK ON THE BRITISH EMPIRE **AND WON!** AND TO DO IT, HE DEVELOPED A NEW AND **RATHER SURPRISING** WEAPON...

PLEASE WELCOME THE FABULOUS **FATHER OF INDIA**...

MOHANDAS "MAHATMA" GANDHI!

MOHANDAS GANDHI
INDIAN ACTIVIST
1869–1948

GANDHI, AS A SMALL BOY IN INDIA, COULD YOU HAVE EVER IMAGINED THAT YOU WOULD GROW UP TO BE ONE OF THE GREATEST **FREEDOM FIGHTERS** OF ALL TIME?

HEE HEE! NO, I DON'T THINK SO! I WAS A VERY **SHY** LITTLE BOY — NOT THE SORT WHO BECOMES A GREAT LEADER!

I USED TO RUN HOME FROM SCHOOL TO AVOID GETTING PICKED ON.

WHEN I FIRST MET MY WIFE (OUR PARENTS ARRANGED IT WHEN I WAS **13**) I WAS TOO SHY TO SPEAK TO HER.

I BECAME A LAWYER, BUT AT MY FIRST CASE, I WAS TOO SHY TO SPEAK IN COURT!

I HAD TO GIVE MY CLIENTS THEIR MONEY BACK AND TELL THEM TO FIND ANOTHER LAWYER!

SO HOW DID YOU FINALLY GET OVER YOUR SHYNESS?

WELL, I TOOK A JOB IN **SOUTH AFRICA**, WHICH MEANT I COULD JUST DO PAPERWORK WITHOUT HAVING TO TALK TO ANYONE...

OR SO I THOUGHT...

I'D ONLY BEEN THERE A WEEK, WHEN I GOT THROWN OFF A TRAIN JUST FOR BEING INDIAN!

CAN'T YOU READ? GET OFF!

THAT MADE ME SO **MAD** THAT I **COULDN'T** KEEP QUIET!

MY FELLOW INDIANS! THIS IS **RUBBISH**!

YEAH, BUT WHAT ARE WE GOING TO DO ABOUT IT?

WHAT **COULD** WE DO!? WE WERE FEW, POOR AND WE HAD NO WEAPONS. WE COULDN'T FIGHT BACK!

BUT YOU HAD A **SECRET WEAPON**!

HEE HEE! IT'S THE **STRONGEST** WEAPON OF ALL! ONE THAT ALWAYS WINS IN THE END...

...LOVE!

WITH LOVE YOU CAN FORGIVE YOUR ENEMIES. LIKE ONE TIME I WAS ATTACKED BY A MOB FOR SPEAKING OUT FOR THE INDIANS...

BUT I REFUSED TO HAVE THEM ARRESTED FOR IT.

HE WHAT!?

PHEW! I WAS WORRIED THERE...

Y'KNOW, MAYBE HE'S NOT SUCH A BAD GUY AFTER ALL...

AND **THAT'S** HOW YOU WIN OVER YOUR ENEMIES AND MAKE THEM YOUR FRIENDS!

YOU RETURNED TO INDIA, DETERMINED TO USE YOUR NEW WEAPON TO MAKE PEOPLE'S LIVES BETTER THERE TOO!

INDIA WAS PART OF THE BRITISH EMPIRE, AND THE BRITISH HAD ALL SORTS OF WAYS TO GET RICH AT OUR EXPENSE.

HO HO

MAN...

THAT'S WHEN I STARTED WEARING THE DHOTI.

THE WHAT?

THIS STYLISH GARMENT. LIKE A BIG NAPPY. INDIANS HAD BEEN WEARING IT FOR CENTURIES.

INSTEAD OF BUYING EXPENSIVE BRITISH CLOTHES, WE COULD JUST MAKE OUR OWN! I ALWAYS LED BY EXAMPLE, SO THAT'S WHAT I DID!

BUT WEARING NAPPIES WASN'T GOING TO GET THE BRITISH OUT OF INDIA! IT WASN'T TIME TO BRING OUT THE BIG GUNS...

NON-COOPERATION!

IF A LAW WAS EVIL AND WRONG, WE'D JUST REFUSE TO FOLLOW IT!

BUT IF YOU BROKE THE LAW, DIDN'T YOU GET PUT IN JAIL?

HEE HEE! ALL THE TIME!

SOON, THERE WERE SO MANY PEOPLE IN JAIL, THEY RAN OUT OF ROOM!

AND OF COURSE, THEY COULD BEAT US AND KILL US, BUT LOVE IS STRONGER THAN FEAR!

PICTURE IT! THOUSANDS OF PEOPLE LINING UP FEARLESSLY TO BE BEATEN.

HEY! NO PUSHING!

THERE'S ENOUGH FOR EVERYONE!

LADIES FIRST!

102

103

THE ART OF NON-VIOLENCE

MOHANDAS "MAHATMA" GANDHI'S PRINCIPLES OF **NON-VIOLENT RESISTANCE** HAVE INSPIRED LEADERS LIKE MARTIN LUTHER KING, NELSON MANDELA AND MANY, MANY OTHERS.

BUT WHAT IS "NON-VIOLENT RESISTANCE"?

THE BASIC PRINCIPLE BEHIND NON-VIOLENCE IS THIS: **ALL LIFE IS ONE.**

SOUNDS LIKE SOME GRAND, COSMIC PROCLAMATION, RIGHT?

AND INDEED IT IS. BUT IT'S ALSO VERY PRACTICAL AND EVERYDAY.

PUBLIC LIBRARY

EVERYTHING GOOD IN OUR LIVES COMES FROM A WEB OF INTERCONNECTED KINDNESS, OF PEOPLE DOING THINGS IN THE HOPE OF HELPING OTHERS.

NON-VIOLENCE IS JUST THE PRINCIPLED APPLICATION OF THAT IDEA IN THE FACE OF HATRED AND INJUSTICE.

NON-VIOLENCE IS **NOT DOING** NOTHING. IT MEANS ACTIVELY SPEAKING **AND ACTING ON** THE TRUTH, WHATEVER THE CONSEQUENCES.

THIS IS NOT A PATH FOR COWARDS - IT CALLS FOR PROFOUND COURAGE, OFTEN IN THE FACE OF VERY REAL DANGER.

THE GOAL IS **NOT** TO DEFEAT OR HUMILIATE PEOPLE, BUT TO AWAKEN THEIR **INNATE GOODNESS.**

REMEMBER, WE ARE FIGHTING EVIL **FORCES** IN SOCIETY, NOT EVIL **PEOPLE.**

SOME PEOPLE SEEM TO BENEFIT FROM INJUSTICE, TO SUPPORT OR EVEN ENACT IT. BUT IT HURTS THEM TOO, SINCE WE ARE ALL CONNECTED.

MY NEXT GUEST IS A **DIFFERENT SORT** OF REBEL: A **FEARLESS FREE SPIRIT** WHOSE **LIFE** IS AS REVOLUTIONARY AS HER ART!

PLEASE MAKE SOME NOISE FOR THE **MONOBROWED MADONNA** OF MEXICAN MODERN ART...

FRIDA KAHLO!

FRIDA KAHLO
MEXICAN ARTIST
1907–1954

FRIDA, YOU ARE TODAY THE WORLD'S MOST FAMOUS AND SUCCESSFUL FEMALE PAINTER. BUT YOU DIDN'T PLAN ON GOING INTO ART AT ALL...

I DIDN'T PLAN ON A LOT OF THINGS, MY FRIEND. BUT LIFE DOESN'T ALWAYS FOLLOW YOUR PLANS.

I **WAS** PLANNING ON BECOMING A **DOCTOR**...

BUT THEN THE BUS I WAS RIDING COLLIDED WITH AN ELECTRIC TROLLEY-CAR.

BROKEN SPINAL COLUMN, BROKEN COLLARBONE, BROKEN RIBS, SHATTERED PELVIS, 11 FRACTURES IN RIGHT LEG, CRUSHED RIGHT FOOT...

IT WAS **MONTHS** BEFORE I COULD EVEN GET OUT OF BED. MY PARENTS BOUGHT ME A PAINTING SET TO KEEP ME OCCUPIED.

PAINTING BECAME MY **SANCTUARY**. AND SINCE I SPENT SO MUCH TIME ALONE, I PAINTED WHAT I KNEW BEST, MYSELF.

YOU ALSO MADE THE, ER... **UNUSUAL** DECISION TO PAINT YOURSELF WITH THE... UH...

THE **WHAT?** THE **MOUSTACHE!?** THE **MONOBROW!?** YOU'RE HARDLY ONE TO TALK!

POINT TAKEN.

ANYWAY, WHAT DO I CARE WHAT SOME IDIOTS THINK? I LOOK THE WAY I LOOK.

AND IT WAS YOUR FEARLESS HONESTY THAT CAUGHT THE EYE OF MEXICO'S MOST FAMOUS ARTIST, THE MURALIST **DIEGO RIVERA**.

AH DIEGO! DIEGO! WHY MUST I LOVE YOU SO!? AI! AI! AI!

UH... **THAT** GUY?

OK, HE WAS OLD, FAT AND UGLY, BUT HE WAS THE GREAT ARTISTIC HERO OF MEXICO. WOMEN **LOVED** HIM.

ACTUALLY, THAT WAS KIND OF THE PROBLEM. WE GOT MARRIED, BUT HE WOULDN'T STOP CHASING OTHER WOMEN.

OH SURE, I LAUGHED, I JOKED, I ACTED LIKE IT WASN'T A BIG DEAL.

BUT IT HURT.

I USED TO SAY, THERE WERE **TWO** ACCIDENTS IN MY LIFE; THE TROLLEY-CAR AND DIEGO, AND DIEGO WAS THE WORST.

NOW **ALL MY LIFE** WAS PAIN. PAIN IN MY SHATTERED BODY, PAIN IN MY BROKEN HEART.

I TRIED DRINKING TO DROWN MY SORROWS, BUT THE DAMN THINGS LEARNED TO SWIM!

ONLY ONE THING HELPED. **PAINTING.**

IF I WAS SPLIT IN TWO BY HEARTBREAK...

OR TORN TO PIECES BY MISCARRIAGES AND UNSUCCESSFUL SURGERIES...

NO MATTER HOW TERRIBLE THE PAIN, IF I COULD PAINT IT, I COULD ENDURE IT.

YOUR SUCCESS GREW AND GREW, AS YOUR HONESTY AND PASSION INSPIRED PEOPLE AROUND THE WORLD.

BUT YOUR HEALTH GOT WORSE AND WORSE UNTIL, DESPITE OVER **30** OPERATIONS, YOU WERE UNABLE TO EVEN GET OUT OF BED.

WHICH IS KIND OF A PROBLEM IF YOU HAVE A **MASSIVE EXHIBITION** OPENING AND YOU CAN'T GO TO YOUR **OWN PARTY!**

WELL, I WASN'T GOING TO LET SOMETHING LIKE **THAT** STOP ME!

KNOCK!
KNOCK!

SO I WENT IN MY JIMMY-JAMS!

YOU MADE A **BED-DAZZLING** ENTRANCE!

¡DIOS MIO!

THE ABOLITION OF SLAVERY HAD BEEN **FORCED** ON THE SOUTHERN STATES AGAINST THEIR WILL AFTER THEY LOST THE AMERICAN CIVIL WAR.

BUT IT WASN'T **REAL** FREEDOM BECAUSE THOSE STATES HAD DEVELOPED A COMPLEX SET OF LOCAL LAWS AND UNWRITTEN CUSTOMS DESIGNED TO KEEP BLACK PEOPLE AS **CLOSE** TO SLAVERY AS THEY COULD GET AWAY WITH.

WE COULDN'T SIT NEXT TO WHITE PEOPLE, COULDN'T SHARE A MEAL WITH THEM, COULDN'T SHAKE HANDS WITH THEM, COULDN'T CALL WHITE PEOPLE BY THEIR FIRST NAME...

HECK, WE COULDN'T EVEN PEE IN THE SAME **TOILET BOWL**!

AND IF THEY **DID** PROVIDE FACILITIES FOR BLACK PEOPLE, THEY WERE ALWAYS THE **CRAPPIEST** IMAGINABLE.

NOT JUST TOILETS EITHER, BUT SCHOOLS, LIBRARIES, HOUSES, JOBS, HEALTHCARE. LITERALLY EVERYTHING YOU COULD THINK OF, OURS WERE WORSE.

AND THERE WERE GANGS OF **TERRORISTS** GOING AROUND BEATING, SHOOTING AND KILLING BLACK PEOPLE FOR THE **TINIEST** BREACH OF THEIR RULES.

I WAS LUCKY - I NEVER EXPERIENCED THAT FIRST-HAND. BUT I REMEMBER SEEING THE BODIES, WHEN I WAS A LITTLE KID.

GOOD GRIEF.

THAT WAS ACTUALLY ONE OF THE MOST EFFECTIVE TOOLS THEY HAD - THE CONSTANT FEAR, AND THE KNOWLEDGE THAT NO ONE WOULD HELP, KEPT US FROM REALISING WE **COULD** STAND UP TO IT.

THAT'S **TERRIBLE**...

BUT YOU KNOW WHAT **REALLY** GOT TO ME?

IT WAS THE LITTLE THINGS...

THE CONSTANT, DAILY REMINDERS THAT WE WEREN'T AS VALUED, RESPECTED OR REALLY EVEN CONSIDERED AS **HUMAN** AS WHITE PEOPLE.

WHITE ONLY

I REMEMBER ONE TIME, I WON A HIGH SCHOOL DEBATING CONTEST...

CONGRATS.

OH, THANKS.

I WAS PRETTY PROUD OF IT. MY WINNING SPEECH WAS ABOUT HOW THE U.S. DECLARATION OF INDEPENDENCE SAYS "ALL MEN ARE CREATED EQUAL" AND HOW IT STILL DIDN'T APPLY TO US.

BUT ON THE WAY HOME, I **STILL** HAD TO GIVE UP MY SEAT WHEN WHITE PASSENGERS GOT ON.

I WAS GOING TO REFUSE, BUT MY TEACHER REMINDED ME IT WAS THE **LAW**. I WOULD'VE GOTTEN ARRESTED. HER TOO, PROBABLY.

I STOOD IN THE AISLE ALL THE WAY HOME. THAT WAS THE **ANGRIEST** I EVER WAS IN MY **LIFE**.

BUT YOU KNOW WHAT INFURIATED ME? MOST WHITE PEOPLE DIDN'T REALLY **NOTICE**! TO THEM IT WAS ALL JUST **NATURAL**.

AFTER ALL, THEY'D BEEN TAUGHT THEIR WHOLE LIVES THAT THEY WERE JUST **MORE IMPORTANT** THAN US.

you're worth it!

AFTER A WHILE, I STOPPED HATING THEM AND STARTED TO **PITY** THEM INSTEAD.

AND FROM PITYING THEM, I CAME TO LOVE AND **FORGIVE** THEM.

REALLY? YOU COULD **FORGIVE** ALL THAT!?

FORGIVENESS DOESN'T MEAN **PUTTING UP** WITH OTHERS' EVIL THOUGHTS OR ACTIONS.

BUT IT **DOES** MEAN MAKING A DISTINCTION BETWEEN EVIL **ACTIONS** AND EVIL **PEOPLE**. EVEN THE BEST PEOPLE HAVE FAULTS, AND I THINK EVEN THE WORST PEOPLE DESERVE A FRESH START, **IF** THEY CHOOSE TO TAKE IT.

SO WHAT CHANGED?

WELL, FIRST OFF, RACISM ISN'T THE ONLY FORM OF INJUSTICE.

I REALISED THAT POOR WHITE PEOPLE WERE BEING TAKEN ADVANTAGE OF TOO, BY RICH BUSINESS OWNERS AND POLITICIANS.

IT'S ALL TOO EASY FOR THE PEOPLE IN POWER TO MAKE LAWS THAT HELP THEMSELVES, AND HURT EVERYBODY ELSE.

OK, HEAR ME OUT ON THIS. HOW ABOUT A MASSIVE TAX CUT... **FOR US!**

THE OTHER THING WAS THE **CHURCH.** I HAD A LOT OF PROBLEMS WITH THE CHURCH, LORD KNOWS, BUT AT THE HEART OF JESUS' TEACHINGS I FOUND THIS WONDERFUL MESSAGE OF LOVE AND FORGIVENESS.

HATE ROTS THE SOUL, BUT LOVE MADE ME FEEL WHOLE AGAIN. I DECIDED TO BECOME A MINISTER, TO SHARE THAT MESSAGE OF LOVE.

AND IT WAS WHILE I WAS TRAINING AS A MINISTER THAT I FIRST HEARD OF THIS AMAZING GUY CALLED **GANDHI** – MAYBE YOU'VE HEARD OF HIM?

THE, UM... THE NAME RINGS A BELL...

GANDHI USED LOVE AND FORGIVENESS LIKE A **WEAPON,** AND HAD COMPLETELY OVERTURNED THE BRITISH EMPIRE IN INDIA.

ONE OF HIS CORE STRATEGIES WAS **CIVIL DISOBEDIENCE,** THE TARGETED BREAKING OF UNJUST LAWS TO GRIND SOCIETY TO A HALT AND FORCE IT TO CONFRONT INJUSTICE.

I THOUGHT A SIMILAR STRATEGY MIGHT WORK IN AMERICA, AND BEGAN BUILDING A NETWORK OF LIKE-MINDED RELIGIOUS MINISTERS AND CIVIL RIGHTS ACTIVISTS.

BUT WE NEEDED A **CAUSE,** A SINGLE INCIDENT SO UNJUST, WE COULD BUILD IT INTO SOMETHING **UN-IGNORABLE.**

AND THEN **ROSA PARKS,** A COURAGEOUS ACTIVIST FROM MONTGOMERY, ALABAMA, DECIDED **NOT** TO GIVE UP HER BUS SEAT, AND GOT ARRESTED.

SHE SAID LATER, SHE DIDN'T **MEAN** TO START A MASSIVE PROTEST. SHE JUST COULDN'T TAKE THE INDIGNITY ANY MORE.

BUT HER DEFIANT ACT WOULD GO ON TO HAVE A MASSIVE EFFECT, PROVIDING THE INCIDENT THAT SPARKED THE CIVIL RIGHTS MOVEMENT!

THE LOCAL ACTIVISTS CALLED A **BOYCOTT** OF THE MONTGOMERY BUS COMPANY, AND THEY ASKED **ME** TO LEAD IT!

UNTIL THE LAW WAS CHANGED TO TREAT US FAIRLY, NO BLACK PERSON WOULD TAKE THE BUS!

HOW DID YOU GET AROUND?

WE WALKED. WE CAR-POOLED. SOME PEOPLE EVEN GOT OUT THEIR OLD HORSE-DRAWN CARTS.

BLACK PEOPLE WERE THE MAJORITY OF BUS CUSTOMERS. SO THE BUS COMPANY WAS GOING **BANKRUPT**, SINCE NO ONE WAS BUYING TICKETS.

BUT THE BOYCOTTERS WERE LOSING MONEY TOO, FROM BEING LATE TO WORK OR GETTING FIRED...

BLACK CHURCHES ALL OVER AMERICA COLLECTED **OLD SHOES** TO SEND TO BOYCOTTERS WHO WERE WEARING OUT THEIR SOLES WITH ALL THAT WALKING!

BUT LOCAL TERRORISTS TRIED TO INTIMIDATE THE BOYCOTTERS, ATTACKING BLACK PEOPLE WALKING TO WORK.

IT ALL CAME DOWN TO WHICH SIDE WOULD GIVE UP FIRST! PART OF MY JOB WAS TO ENCOURAGE AND INSPIRE THE BOYCOTTERS, AS WELL AS EXPLAINING OUR GOALS TO THE WIDER WORLD.

AND YOU KNOW WHAT, WE WERE **WINNING**! OUR CAMPAIGN GOT MASSIVE NATIONAL NEWS COVERAGE THAT TURNED THE TIDE OF PUBLIC OPINION.

ROSA PARKS' CASE GOT BUMPED UP TO A FEDERAL COURT, WHICH RULED THAT THE SEPARATE BUS SEATS THING WAS **UNCONSTITUTIONAL** (AND THEREFORE ILLEGAL).

AFTER **381** GRUELLING DAYS, THE BUS COMPANY WAS FORCED TO ABANDON SEGREGATION AND LET PEOPLE SIT WHERE THEY LIKED!

SOUNDS LIKE THE BOYCOTT WORKED...

WELL, YES AND NO. I MEAN, WE **WON**. BUT A LOT OF PEOPLE WERE **NOT** HAPPY ABOUT IT...

THE TERRORISTS RAMPED UP THEIR VIOLENT CAMPAIGN, SHOOTING INTO BUSES AND BLOWING UP CHURCHES.

MY GOD. THAT REALLY **IS** TERRIFYING.

TERROR WAS REALLY THE ONLY TOOL THEY HAD LEFT. WHAT **WE** HAD TO DO WAS **REFUSE TO BE SCARED.**

AND THAT WASN'T EASY AT FIRST – WE HAD TO TRAIN NON-VIOLENT PROTESTORS IN HOW TO TAKE A BEATING **WITHOUT** RUNNING **OR** FIGHTING BACK. THAT TAKES REAL COURAGE.

BUT LOOK, IT WAS A START. ONE THING I REALLY NOTICED WAS THE POWER OF A NEW INVENTION THAT WAS SWEEPING AMERICA: **TELEVISION!**

TV MADE IT HARDER FOR THE REST OF AMERICA TO KEEP TURNING A BLIND EYE.

AND IT HELPED BLACK PEOPLE SEE THAT BY WORKING TOGETHER, WE ACTUALLY **COULD** MAKE A DIFFERENCE.

NON-VIOLENT PROTESTS BEGAN SPRINGING UP ALL OVER THE PLACE, WITH THOUSANDS OF COURAGEOUS ACTIVISTS RISKING ARREST, INJURY AND EVEN DEATH FOR WHAT THEY BELIEVED.

THEY HELD **SIT-INS** WHERE BLACK PROTESTORS WOULD SIT IN THE "WHITE ONLY" SECTIONS OF RESTAURANTS, PARKS, EVEN LIBRARIES...

SHH!

WHITE ONLY

THEY HELD **KNEEL-INS,** WHERE BLACK WORSHIPPERS JOINED WHITE-ONLY CHURCH SERVICES...

LET'S SEE HOW **CHRISTIAN** YOU ARE **NOW**...

AND THEY HELD **MARCHES** AND **RALLIES** TO CALL FOR BLACK VOTING RIGHTS, EQUAL TREATMENT AND AN END TO POLICE BRUTALITY.

END segregation NOW!

CIVIL RIGHTS ARE HUMAN RIGHTS

LOCAL GOVERNMENTS TRIED PASSING LAWS MAKING **ALL** FORMS OF PROTEST ILLEGAL, BUT WE CALLED THEIR BLUFF, CRAMMING THEIR JAILS TO **BURSTING.**

IN SOME PLACES, POLICE EMPLOYED EXTRAORDINARY **BRUTALITY,** USING WATER CANNONS, BILLY CLUBS AND ATTACK DOGS TO DISBAND MARCHERS.

IT WAS HORRIFIC. BUT IT WAS **ALSO** ALL OVER THE NEWS. NOW **NO ONE** COULD IGNORE THE INJUSTICES WE LIVED EVERY DAY.

INSPIRED BY THE PROTESTORS' COURAGE, AND EMBARRASSED BY THE INTERNATIONAL OUTRAGE, PRESIDENT **JOHN F. KENNEDY** STARTED CALLING FOR CIVIL RIGHTS REFORMS.

ALONG WITH ALMOST A QUARTER OF A **MILLION** PROTESTORS, YOU MARCHED ON THE CAPITOL TO PUT YOUR DEMANDS TO THE PRESIDENT.

IT WAS THERE, IN FRONT OF THE LARGEST DEMONSTRATION IN U.S. HISTORY UP TO THAT POINT, YOU DELIVERED THE SPEECH OF A LIFETIME.

BLASTING THE HYPOCRISY OF RACIST OPPRESSION, WHILE ALSO PAINTING A MOVING PICTURE OF WHAT A COUNTRY **WITHOUT** RACISM MIGHT LOOK LIKE, YOUR **"I HAVE A DREAM"** SPEECH BECAME ONE OF THE MOST FAMOUS OF THE MODERN AGE.

I HAVE A DREAM THAT MY FOUR LITTLE CHILDREN WILL ONE DAY LIVE IN A NATION WHERE THEY WILL NOT BE JUDGED BY THE COLOUR OF THEIR SKIN BUT BY THE CONTENT OF THEIR CHARACTER.

IT WAS THE TURNING OF THE TIDE. OVER THE NEXT FEW YEARS, THE GOVERNMENT PASSED A SERIES OF RADICAL NEW LAWS, BANNING ALL FORMS OF SEGREGATION AND GUARANTEEING BLACK PEOPLES' RIGHT TO VOTE.

YOU WON THE **NOBEL PEACE PRIZE** FOR YOUR EFFORTS, AND WERE ALSO NAMED **TIME** MAGAZINE'S **MAN OF THE YEAR.**

SO HAD YOU ACCOMPLISHED YOUR DREAM?

HM.

AGAIN, YES AND NO.

THOSE NEW LAWS MADE SEPARATE BUS SEATS, SCHOOLS, HOSPITALS AND ALL THE REST **ILLEGAL**, AND THAT WAS A BIG DEAL, DON'T MISTAKE ME.

AND WE EFFECTIVELY ENDED THE REIGN OF TERROR IN THE SOUTH. FACED WITH INCREASED SCRUTINY, STATE GOVERNMENTS STARTED CLAMPING DOWN ON DOMESTIC TERRORISTS.

WHAT IS THIS, MAN? I THOUGHT YOU WERE ON OUR SIDE!

AND ALL THOSE PROTESTORS WHO TOOK A BEATING OR WENT TO JAIL, AND CAME OUT THE OTHER END SINGING FREEDOM SONGS, WENT HOME RADICALLY CHANGED.

BUT RACISM AND INJUSTICE DIDN'T JUST GO AWAY. I BEGAN TO REALISE RACISM COULDN'T BE FOUGHT ON ITS OWN – WE HAD TO LOOK AT THE UNJUST SOCIETY THAT PRODUCED IT.

HOW CAN AMERICA, OR ANY OTHER RICH COUNTRY FOR THAT MATTER, HAVE **SO MANY** PEOPLE WHO CAN'T AFFORD FOOD, A HOME OR THE OTHER BASIC NECESSITIES OF A DIGNIFIED LIFE?

I BEGAN MY MOST AMBITIOUS CAMPAIGN YET, A COALITION OF BLACK **AND** WHITE PEOPLE, DEMANDING A RADICAL RESTRUCTURING OF SOCIETY TO PUT **PEOPLE** BEFORE **PROFITS**.

BUT BEFORE YOU COULD GET IT OFF THE GROUND YOU WERE ASSASSINATED BY A RACIST CRIMINAL WHO HAD ESCAPED FROM PRISON THE YEAR BEFORE.

IT'S JUST SO **UNFAIR**! YOU SPENT YOUR WHOLE LIFE WORKING TO MAKE THE WORLD A BETTER PLACE.

AND SOME BITTER IDIOT WITH A GUN CAN JUST END IT LIKE THAT!

OK, BUT LOOK, THERE WILL **ALWAYS** BE UNSCRUPULOUS PEOPLE WHO WHIP UP HATE AND FEAR TO WIN POWER.

SOMETIMES THEY'LL EVEN WIN, FOR A WHILE. BUT AS I ONCE SAID...

I BELIEVE THAT UNARMED TRUTH AND UNCONDITIONAL LOVE WILL HAVE THE FINAL WORD IN REALITY. THIS IS WHY RIGHT, TEMPORARILY DEFEATED, IS STRONGER THAN EVIL TRIUMPHANT.

MORE
CORPSE TALK
AVAILABLE
NOW!

OUT NOW!

CORPSE TALK
Ground-Breaking
SCIENTISTS

Adam & Lisa Murphy

How did a **TASTE** of **TORTOISE** inspire **DARWIN'S** discoveries?

What led **EINSTEIN** t~~o~~ the secrets of **SPACE**

What~~'s~~ ~~the de~~al with **MARIE CURIE** ~~DE~~ADLY **DIARIES?**

How did ELIZABETH I SMASH the SPANISH ARMADA?

How did ANNE FRANK'S DIARY help her DEAL with DESPAIR?

Was CHING SHIH the world's COOLEST PIRATE QUEEN?

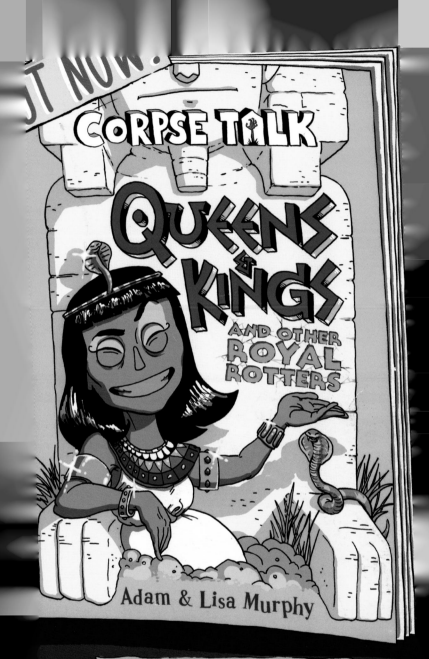

CORPSE TALK

QUEENS & KINGS

AND OTHER ROYAL ROTTERS

Adam & Lisa Murphy

How did CLEOPATRA'S CARPET make a GRAND ENTRANCE?

What was behind HENRY VIII's TOURNAMENT TRIUMPHS?

RICHARD THE LIONHEART: HERO KING or ROYAL REPROBATE?